HAROLD PINT

The Birthday Party

With a Commentary and Chronology by
PATRICIA HERN

and Notes by
GLENDA LEEMING

Methuen Student Editions
EYRE METHUEN · LONDON

This Methuen Student Edition first published in 1981 by Eyre
Methuen Ltd, 11 New Fetter Lane, London EC4P 4EE.
The Birthday Party first published in 1960 by Methuen & Co.
Revised second edition, 1965.
The Birthday Party copyright © 1959, 1960 and 1965 by
Harold Pinter
Commentary and Notes copyright © 1981 by Eyre Methuen
Printed in Great Britain by Fakenham Press Ltd, Fakenham,
Norfolk

ISBN O 413 39640 1

*Thanks are due to James Gibbs, Malcolm Page and Non Worrall
for their help and advice in the preparation of this edition.*

Contents

Six pages of illustrations appear at the end of the Commentary after page xxx.

Contents

Harold Pinter

1930 10 October. Pinter was born into a Jewish family in Hackney, an inner suburb in East London. His father was a tailor, and the family lived in a comfortable terraced house. Nonetheless, the consciousness of being Jewish and thus one of a vulnerable group must have been sharpened by the activities during the 1930s of Oswald Mosley and his British Union of Fascists.

1939 He was evacuated to Cornwall, returning eventually to London in 1944, where he attended Hackney Downs Grammar School, displaying a particular enthusiasm for English and the theatre.

1948 He gained a grant to attend the Royal Academy of Dramatic Art, but was unhappy there and left before the end of his first year.

1948 -49 Pinter was called up for National Service in the Armed Forces, but, with the fight against Fascism over, he declared himself a conscientious objector. Two tribunals rejected his appeal for exemption, but instead of a prison sentence he escaped with a fine. After taking part in a few radio plays, he went back to drama school, this time at the Central School of Speech and Drama.

1951 -52 Pinter was taken on by the actor-manager Anew McMaster for a Shakespearian tour of Ireland. During this period he published a number of poems.

1952 -56 Pinter acted in provincial repertory theatre, marrying actress Vivien Merchant in 1956.

1957 His first play, *The Room,* was produced by Bristol University Drama Department, then by the Bristol Old Vic Theatre School whose production brought Pinter to the attention of a theatre producer, Michael Codron.

1958 Michael Codron bought an option on Pinter's second play, *The Birthday Party.* In April, *The Birthday Party* was performed at the Arts Theatre in Cambridge, toured to Oxford, Wolverhampton and Brighton, then, in May, opened at the Lyric Theatre, Hammersmith, in West

London. It closed after only one week, having been savaged by the critics. Only Harold Hobson, drama critic of the Sunday Times, recognised Pinter's quality.

> Mr. Pinter, on the evidence of this work, possesses the most original, disturbing and arresting talent in theatrical London. [. . .] Theatrically speaking *The Birthday Party* is absorbing. It is witty. [. . .] Mr. Pinter has got hold of a primary fact of existence. We live on the verge of disaster.

That winter Pinter wrote another full-length play, *The Hothouse,* but, perhaps discouraged by the initial reception of *The Birthday Party,* he did not submit it for production until 1980.

1959   *The Birthday Party* was performed more successfully by a semi-professional company, the Tavistock Players, at the Tower Theatre in London, and Pinter's radio play, *A Slight Ache,* was broadcast by the BBC.

1960   *The Room* and *The Dumb Waiter* were produced at the Hampstead Theatre Club, later transferring to the Royal Court Theatre. *A Night Out* was broadcast on radio.

1960   April: *The Caretaker* at the Arts Theatre Club won sufficient critical acclaim to justify its transfer to the Duchess Theatre in the West End, where it ran for a year. *Night School* was televised and another production of *The Birthday Party* opened — this time, in America.

1961   *The Collection* was televised by ATV. *The Caretaker* opened in New York and won good notices.

1962   Pinter wrote the screenplay for Joseph Losey's film of Robin Maugham's novel, *The Servant,* winning the British Screenwriters' Guild Award. *The Caretaker* was filmed.

1963   *The Lover* was televised.

1964   Revival of *The Birthday Party* by the Royal Shakespeare Company at the Aldwych Theatre in June. Directed by Pinter.

1965   Pinter won a British Film Academy Award for his screenplay of Penelope Mortimer's novel, *The Pumpkin Eater. The Homecoming* was presented by the Royal Shakespeare Company at the Aldwych Theatre, London.

1966   The film of Pinter's screenplay, *The Quiller Memorandum,* was directed by Michael Anderson. Pinter was awarded the C.B.E. in the Queen's Birthday Honours List.

CHRONOLOGY

1967 *The Basement* was televised by BBC-TV. Pinter wrote the screenplay for Losey's film of *Accident*, a novel by Nicholas Mosley. *The Homecoming* won the Tony Award for the best play on Broadway.

1968 *The Birthday Party* was filmed. Director: William Friedkin.

1969 Pinter completed his adaptation of L.P. Hartley's novel, *The Go-Between*, as a film to be directed by Joseph Losey. Two one-act plays, *Landscape* and *Silence*, were produced by the Royal Shakespeare Company at the Aldwych Theatre. The production on stage of *Landscape* had been delayed because Pinter refused to make the cuts in the text required by the Lord Chamberlain's Office, then still exercising censorship over live theatre. An uncut version of the play, however, had been broadcast on BBC radio in January, 1968.

1971 *Old Times* was presented by the Royal Shakespeare Company at the Aldwych Theatre.

1972 Pinter began work on an adaptation for the screen of Proust's *A la Recherche du Temps Perdu*.

1973 Pinter became an Associate Director at the National Theatre. His short play, *Monologue*, was televised by the BBC.

1975 *No Man's Land* was produced by the National Theatre Company at the Old Vic Theatre, then transferred to the West End, and later was staged in the new National Theatre on London's South Bank.

1978 *Betrayal* opened at the National Theatre.

1980 *The Hothouse*, written in 1958, was directed by Pinter at the Hampstead Theatre, then transferred to the Ambassador's Theatre in the West End. Pinter completed his screenplay of John Fowles' novel, *The French Lieutenant's Woman*. His first marriage ended in divorce; he married Lady Antonia Fraser.

1981 *Family Voices* was broadcast on BBC radio and subsequently staged as a Platform Performance at the National Theatre.

Pinter has also directed several of his own plays and plays by other dramatists for the stage and for television, developing a particularly fruitful working relationship with the playwright, Simon Gray.

Plays in order of writing:

The Room; The Birthday Party; The Dumb Waiter; A Slight Ache; The Hothouse; A Night Out; The Caretaker; Night School; The Dwarfs; The Collection; The Lover; Tea Party; The Homecoming; The Basement; Landscape; Silence; Night; Old Times; Monologue; No Man's Land; Betrayal; Family Voices.

Screenplays from other writers' work:
The Servant; The Pumpkin Eater; The Quiller Memorandum; Accident; The Go-Between; Langrishe, Go Down; The Last Tycoon; A la Recherche du Temps Perdu (not filmed); *The French Lieutenant's Woman.*

Plays directed for the stage:
The Collection; The Lover; The Dwarfs; The Birthday Party; The Man in the Glass Booth by Robert Shaw; *Exiles* by James Joyce; *Butley* by Simon Gray; *Next of Kin* by John Hopkins; *Otherwise Engaged* by Simon Gray; *Blithe Spirit* by Noël Coward; *The Innocents* by William Archibald; *The Rear Column* by Simon Gray; *Close of Play* by Simon Gray; *The Hothouse; Quartermaine's Terms* by Simon Gray.

Plot

The action of the play is, on the surface, simple, because uncomplicated by a sub-plot.

Act I

Stanley Webber, a one-time pianist in a sea-side concert party and now in his late thirties, is in retreat — from what is not clear — at the seedy boarding-house run by Meg with the passive support of her husband, Petey. Meg is in her sixties, sentimental and unintelligent. She dotes on Stanley, trying to be both mother and mistress to him, smothering him with playful, clumsily flirtatious affection, despite his obvious contempt for her. Two strangers arrive, Goldberg and McCann; they have a job to do, a job which makes McCann uneasy. Stan's reaction to their arrival suggests that he has been expecting and dreading this moment. He slinks out of the back door to avoid them. Meg is delighted by the idea that her boarding-house is 'on the list'. Encouraged by Goldberg's flattery, she tells them what she knows about Stanley. When she declares that it is Stanley's birthday, Goldberg and McCann suggest that they organise a party for him that evening. On his return, she proudly presents Stanley with a toy drum, bought with the assistance of Lulu, a young neighbour whose advances Stanley peevishly resists. Meg hopes that the drum will somehow revive Stanley's interest in music and make him content to stay with her. He begins to play the drum, gently at first, then with an uncontrolled frenzy.

Act II

That evening Stanley, evidently frightened, tries to discover who Goldberg and McCann are and what they want; he alternately blusters and wheedles, always insisting that he is not the man they are after, and that, if he is, he has not done whatever it is they are after him for. Goldberg and McCann subject him to a strange and destructive interrogation during which they render him effectively blind by removing his glasses. Meg's appearance, in evening dress and playing the drum, interrupts the growing violence between

Stanley and his two tormentors. The party begins. Stanley remains silently brooding while Meg grows increasingly sentimental, encouraged by Goldberg. Stanley's isolation is emphasised when Lulu arrives and begins a heavy flirtation with Goldberg while Meg and McCann, relaxed by whiskey, talk of happy times they think they remember. The mood changes when a game of blind-man's-buff begins. Again Stanley has to surrender his glasses; he is blindfolded. As he gropes his way slowly forwards, McCann places the drum in his path so that Stan catches his foot in it and moves on, dragging the drum with him. He reaches Meg and tries to strangle her. As Goldberg and McCann pull him away the lights suddenly go out and, in the confusion of darkness, panic grows, heightened by a series of grunts, an insistent drum beat, and, as a climax, a scream from Lulu. The light of McCann's torch shows Stan leaning over Lulu, who is spread-eagled on the table. With the light in his eyes, Stan retreats against a wall, giggling, while Goldberg and McCann close in on him.

Act III

The following morning Meg, suffering a hangover, goes out to buy food, leaving Petey at home. Petey is worried about Stanley, but Goldberg's answers to his questions are evasive and do nothing to reassure him. McCann enters with suitcases. He, too, is uneasy, apparently disturbed by the hours he has spent with Stan during the night. Goldberg tries to be assertive and assured, but he finds himself at a loss for the right words and in need of comfort from McCann. Evidently this job has been unlike other assignments. Goldberg regains some of his old assurance when Lulu comes in to reproach him for seducing her the night before. He refuses to take her air of injured innocence seriously. McCann frightens her by insisting that she is a wicked woman who needs to confess her faults. She retreats, muttering that she knows what has been going on, that she has seen what has been happening. When McCann brings Stanley in, the change is startling: Stanley is now neatly dressed in a dark suit and white shirt; he appears stunned and withdrawn. In his hands he holds his broken glasses. Goldberg and McCann promise him a golden future; he is to be taken care of, made a success. In reply, he can only grunt and gasp painfully. As Goldberg and McCann begin to hustle Stanley towards the door, Petey comes in and tries to rouse Stanley into resistance or, failing that, to protect him from whatever it is that Goldberg and McCann are taking him to face, but when they suggest that he, too, come with them to see Monty, whoever *he* is, Petey's nerve fails and he allows Stanley to be taken away. Meg returns, unaware of what has happened; Petey shrinks from telling her, so the play ends with her happy memories of what a wonderful party it had been. With unconscious irony, she insists (page 87):

MEG: It was a lovely party. I haven't laughed so much for years. We had dancing and singing. And games. You should have been there.
PETEY: It was good, eh?

Pause

MEG: I was the belle of the ball.
PETEY: Were you?
MEG: Oh yes. They all said I was.
PETEY: I bet you were, too.
MEG: Oh, it's true. I was.

Pause

I know I was.

Commentary

What kind of play — tragedy or comedy?

What kind of play is *The Birthday Party?* How is it organised? The play has the built-in tension of any hunting story: in Act I we see the fugitive gone to ground, uneasily awaiting discovery; we see the hunters arrive and scent out their quarry. As soon as both parties have been identified, the excitement lies not in any kind of detective work for the audience, but in the thrill of the chase itself. At no point is there any real prospect of Stanley escaping. In Act II he tries to dodge and evade capture, then, like an animal at bay, he turns on his pursuers in violent but futile desperation. In Act III the hunters depart with their prize neatly trussed and dressed to be served up to the mysterious Monty.

So there is tension, a kind of excitement. That does not, however, answer the question — what kind of play? Tragedy or comedy? *The Birthday Party* has an almost conventional structure; that is to say, it has a recognisable beginning, a middle, and an end. Act I contains the exposition, introducing the characters, demonstrating their relationship to each other, and announcing the event, the party itself, which will move the plot forwards. Act II builds quickly to the dramatic climax, the moment of explicit crisis and conflict when Stan attacks and is attacked and after which nothing will ever be quite the same. Act III shows the repercussions of that event: the characters have all been changed by the experience. Stan is past action; the crisis for him has been resolved. There is no longer any suspense, but rather the satisfaction of seeing the pattern completed.

The pattern is a familiar one; it can be seen in one of the most influential forms of early drama, Greek tragedy — for example, in the trilogy, *The Oresteia,* by Aeschylus. The middle play of this trilogy shows a society ill at ease, living under the rule of Aegisthus and of Queen Clytemnestra, who had killed her husband, Agamemnon, on his return from Troy. The arrival of Orestes, Clytemnestra's exiled son, violently disturbs this uneasy calm, as, spurred on by his sister, Electra, he hunts down and kills his mother, Clytemnestra, and then is forced to run away, pursued by the Furies who will drive him mad unless Apollo can save him. When Orestes departs, bearing his guilt with him, the others are left to pick up what remains of their routine existence, to establish a semblance at least of normality, despite having been deeply affected by the tragic events. Life must go on. The drama works within specific limits — the Unities of Time, Place and Action. That is to say there is one plot-line, the action does not move from city to city, and exists within a time-limit of about twenty-four hours. Not only does this give this and other Greek plays the concentration and clarity which partly explain their continuing impact, but it can also be intellectually and aesthetically satisfying, not straining the tolerance and imaginative elasticity of the audience. Traditionally no bloodshed occurred within sight of the audience, although the language could be violent, and the effects of bloodshed could be vividly shown.

The Birthday Party can also be seen to operate within these conventions: the action has a single strand and is contained within the walls of Meg's boarding house between one morning and the next; there is no blood spilt on stage — the sense of impending catastrophe is, on the whole, conveyed through the language and through certain almost ritualistic actions (the game of blind-man's-buff, for example). The play opens on a scene of normality, troubled only by Stanley's nervousness and a sense that all is not as it appears to be. This is disturbed by the introduction of an element from outside — Goldberg and McCann — which leads to a dramatic crisis, a shocking event. Then the intruders leave, carrying guilt or responsibility with them, while the others have to go on living as best they can. There is a relentless progress towards the 'tragic' climax; Stanley seems, despite his frantic denials, to recognise his guilt for some undefined crime and very soon admits the futility of struggling against what might be seen as the forces of retribution, the Furies here being represented by Goldberg and McCann, who have the power to destroy his mind, if not to kill him bodily.

If one takes a common view of the distinction between tragedy and comedy — that tragedy presents a crisis or conflict to which there is no happy solution, only the inevitable destruction of the protagonist, whereas comedy presents a crisis or confusion to which the audience is always confident there is a happy solution — then *The Birthday Party* still appears as a tragedy. Even though Stanley is not seen deliberately to choose the path to tragic retribution, to initiate a chain of events culminating in his own destruction as, say, Shakespeare's Macbeth does, nevertheless his suffering is not accidental; he suffers because he is who he is, caught in a situation which he cannot escape. What happens to him, therefore, has a particular significance; it happens for a reason, not in a haphazard, casual way. Arguably Stanley lacks stature for a tragic hero; there is no spectacle of a great man's fall. Another leading playwright of this century, Arthur Miller, tried to find a view of tragedy, and of the nature of the tragic hero, which had some relevance to a society no longer bound closely to the fates of princes and warriors. He suggested that the social status of the hero matters little in itself, that the hero is raised to tragic stature by the unusual intensity of his feelings and by his inability to walk away from the dangers and pain implicit in his situation. It is interesting that Stanley does not simply disappear when Goldberg and McCann arrive, although he is able to slip out of the back door and could, therefore, run away from trouble. He is somehow compelled to return to complete the action, to suffer a kind of death. The intensity of his feelings is conveyed partly through his frenzied drumming, partly through his collapse under interrogation, and partly through his sudden, desperate bursts of violence. More eloquent, perhaps, is his inability to speak or to act in the final scene.

'Comedy of Menace'?

'Tragedy' is not, however, the label most commonly attached to *The Birthday Party*. The play is more often described as a 'Comedy of Menace' — a description not originally coined for Pinter, but now primarily associated with his early plays. What does the term imply? A particular quality of response from the audience, the uneasy laughter that comes from nervousness, the laughter by which the audience tries to demonstrate that there is a safe distance between themselves and what they see or hear happening in the play. Pinter explained this response in relation to *The Caretaker*, but his comments seem equally applicable here.

> But where the comic and the tragic (for want of a better word) are closely interwoven, certain members of the audience will always give emphasis to the comic as opposed to the other, for by so doing they rationalise the other out of existence . . . This laughter is in fact a mode of precaution, a smoke screen, a refusal to accept what is happening as recognisable (which I think it is) and instead to view the actors (a) as actors always and not as characters and (b) as chimpanzees.

'Menace' feeds on people's acceptance, no matter how reluctant, of the possibility that danger or disaster lurks round the next corner, hidden as yet, and therefore all the more unnerving. The connection between the characters' predicament and the audience's private anxieties must be strongly established, or there will be no menace felt, no reason for the defensive laughter. The audience laughs at Meg's childish terror at Stan's description of the men who will come in a van, that very day (page 24):

STAN: And do you know what they've got in that van?
MEG: What?
STAN: They've got a wheelbarrow in that van.
MEG (breathlessly): They haven't.
STAN: Oh yes they have.
MEG: You're a liar.
STAN (advancing upon her): A big wheelbarrow. And when the van stops they wheel it out, and they wheel it up the garden path, and they they knock at the front door.
MEG: They don't.
STAN: They're looking for someone.
MEG: They're not.
STAN: They're looking for someone. A certain person.
MEG (hoarsely): No, they're not!
STAN: Shall I tell you who they're looking for?
MEG: No!
STAN: You don't want me to tell you?
MEG: You're a liar!

Laughter proclaims that the audience is too sophisticated, too aware, to be so gullible. Yet there can be few who have not at some time, even in adult life, been startled by a chill of fear at what seems on the surface to be trivial. The purposeful arrival of men in an unmarked van, or big black car, 'looking for someone', has long been a potent image in American and European cinema. The threat need not be explicit; the power of suggestion is important — shades of prison vans, mafia limousines, undertakers' hearses, the secret police. So that the laughter which on one level asserts the audience's separateness from Stan or Meg, on a different level is an admission of kinship.

Irony is one way in which the relationship between an appearance of normality and a sense of impending catastrophe operates; the audience mocks the characters' ignorance of the real significance of a word or phrase or action. Pinter uses this device repeatedly in *The Birthday Party*. This is perhaps one reason why the play has grown in popularity as it has become more familiar — the sustained tension needs a level of awareness, of foreknowledge, which was certainly not there at its first performances in 1958. For example, in Act I Meg is enthusiastic about the idea of a party for Stan (page 33):

> MEG: Oh, this is going to cheer Stanley up. It will, He's been down in the dumps lately.
> GOLDBERG: We'll bring him out of himself.

The peculiar frisson, the perhaps rueful smile, which Goldberg's reply can excite depends upon one's vivid idea of just how drastically Goldberg and McCann are going to bring Stanley 'out of himself'.

Foreknowledge of the plot is not necessary for an appreciation of the ironies conveyed through the shifts of meaning within a single phrase. These create tensions and uncertainties which have come to be part of what is meant by the term 'Pinteresque'. When Meg, for example, tries to give Goldberg and McCann an account of Stanley's past triumphs, she echoes Stanley's words but alters the sense. Stan's version (page 23):

> STAN: Champagne we had that night, the lot. (*Pause.*) My father nearly came down to hear me. [. . .] Then after that, you know what they did? They carved me up. Carved me up. [. . .] They pulled a fast one. I'd like to know who was responsible for that. (*Bitterly.*) All right, Jack, I can take a tip. They want me to crawl down on my bended knees. Well, I can take a tip . . . any day of the week.

Meg's version (page 32):

> MEG: [. . .] They were very grateful. (*Pause.*) And then they all wanted to give him a tip. And so he took the tip. And then he got a fast train and he came down here.

Meg's rose-tinted misinterpretation of Stanley's story is absurd; the audience can laugh at her sentimental foolishness. There is also pleasure in acknowledging Pinter's exploitation of the critical difference in meaning between 'take a tip' and 'give a tip'. Puns, or word play, are part of a long-standing tradition of English humour, but here there is also the more serious recognition that this is merely one example of how language makes 'truthful' communication difficult, tending rather to emphasise a character's isolation. Stanley has tried to describe an experience which was full of horror and bitterness for him; Meg has listened, anxious to share Stanley's memories as a way of binding him to her, yet has failed to understand his words, hearing only what she wanted to hear.

Comedy comes also from the statement of the obvious — as in the exchange between Meg and Petey (page 9):

MEG: Is that you, Petey?

> *Pause*

Petey, is that you?

> *Pause*

Petey?
PETEY: What?
MEG: Is that you?
PETEY: Yes, it's me.
MEG: What? (*Her face appears at the hatch.*) Are you back?
PETEY: Yes.

Or from the banality of the conversation which has to fill the empty space between characters whose lives are emotionally or intellectually impoverished. Snippets from newspaper gossip columns give Meg vicarious delight (page 11):

MEG: What are you reading?
PETEY: Someone's just had a baby.
MEG: Oh, they haven't! Who?
PETEY: Some girl.
MEG: Who, Petey, who?
PETEY: I don't think you'd know her.
MEG: What's her name?
PETEY: Lady Mary Splatt.
MEG: I don't know her.

Apart from Meg's ingenuous surprise over what is a commonplace event, there is the absurdity of the name: Lady Mary (redolent of aristocratic gentility) Splatt (suddenly suggestive of slapstick vulgarity). The sharp descent from the sublime to the ridiculous, or from the apparently profound to the banal, occurs often in the play. Stanley reminisces about a concert he claims to have given. 'It was a good one, too. They were all there that night. Every single one of them. It was a great success. Yes. A concert.' Such a concert should happen in a concert hall of repute, in the heart of

London's cultural campus. 'It was a great success. Yes. A concert. At Lower Edmonton.' 'Lower' emphasises the suburban ordinariness of Edmonton – the bathos is both comic and an important comment on Stanley's character.

Character or caricature?

Comedy in *The Birthday Party* comes not only from the patterns of language but from the clichés and contradictions within the characters themselves. Here, too, there is a tension between the well-worn comic stereotypes and an underlying insecurity or sense of danger. At first glance, Pinter seems to present the audience with a set of stock characters, the staple diet served up in popular comedy sketches. They are instantly classifiable, basically static, or, to use E.M. Forster's term, 'flat', unlikely to surprise anyone. There is the hard-headed Jew, affectedly sentimental; the whiskey-drinking, potentially violent religious bigot of an Irishman; the placid, uncommunicative deck-chair attendant; the buxom, amorous girl called Lulu; and the silly, seedy landlady whose fried bread is a source of pride and whose tea is like gravy. The dialogue makes clear, sharp outlines, using the caricaturist's device of simplification, over-statement and repetition (page 43):

> GOLDBERG: Humming away I'd be, past the children's playground. I'd tip my hat to the toddlers, I'd give a helping hand to a couple of stray dogs, everything came natural. I can see it like yesterday. The sun falling behind the dog stadium. Ah! [. . .] Up the street, into my gate, inside the door, home. 'Simey!' my old mum used to shout, 'quick before it gets cold.' And there on the table what would I see? The nicest piece of gefilte fish you could wish to find on a plate.

The encounters between different stereotypes can be funny, as one type thoughtlessly applies inappropriate standards to the other (page 29):

> McCANN: Yes, it's true, you've done a lot for me. I appreciate it.
> GOLDBERG: Say no more.
> McCANN: You've always been a true Christian.
> GOLDBERG: In a way.

Clichés or stock characters are a kind of dramatic shorthand: Goldberg stands not just as one man, but as the embodiment of a widely held set of preconceptions about being Jewish, including a sense of guilt amongst Gentiles — 'you betrayed our breed.' However, the character of Goldberg also has a depth and vitality which make him more than a flat cliché. In his poem, 'A View of the Party', written in 1958 and reprinted in Pinter's *Poems and Prose 1949-1977* (London, Eyre Methuen, 1977), Pinter sets Goldberg at the centre of the play, a man carrying within his past threads that tie all the characters of *The Birthday Party* together.

> The thought that Goldberg was
> A man she might have known
> Never crossed Meg's words
> That morning in the room [. . .]

> The thought that Goldberg was
> Sat in the centre of the room,
> A man of weight and time,
> To supervise the game.

Goldberg is both a 'thought' and 'A man of weight and time' — not simply a stereotype, an abstraction; he is something more physical, more frightening, yet with the enduring and pervasive charm of a provocative idea.

Similarly, McCann carries with him a complex assortment of historical, religious, political and folk-based traditions. Ireland is commonly associated with explosive religious fervour, drunken rhetoric, a sense of national grievance, sentimental patriotism, easy violence. McCann is said to be a defrocked priest, is seen drinking Irish whiskey and becoming lyrically homesick, as well as heard challenging Stanley to answer for England's brutality to Ireland in the past. Yet he, like Goldberg, cannot satisfactorily be explained in terms of comic or racial stereotypes. This is demonstrated when Stanley tries to ingratiate himself with McCann by offering him a generalised view of Ireland and the Irish as he thinks the Irish would like to be seen (page 42):

> STANLEY: I know Ireland very well. I've many friends there.
> I love that country and I admire and trust its people. I trust
> them. They respect the truth and they have a sense of
> humour. I think their policemen are wonderful. I've been
> there. I've never seen such sunsets. What about coming out
> to have a drink with me? There's a pub down the road serves
> draught Guinness.

The clichés seem thin and absurd in the face of the real McCann.

It is the presence of Stanley that brings into focus the more disturbing and complicated features of the others. He is the cause of Goldberg's and McCann's arrival at Meg's boarding-house; he brings them together, setting up tensions and frictions between them as they carry out this distasteful assignment, 'the job' McCann feels so unhappy about and which momentarily makes Goldberg lose his self-assurance. His past — whatever the truth of it is — contains the key to the events of the play itself. He first sounds the note of alarm, cutting through the apparently trivial chatter of Meg. From the beginning he is aware of the vulnerability of his retreat, aware that the threat will come from outside, communicating his fear to the audience. The abrupt change of tone when he hears of the two strangers who are about to violate his sanctuary, his evasiveness in the face of direct questions, his willingness to submit to the sticky caresses of someone twice his age and with half his intelligence, all combine to create suspense and to make the audience ready to accept the idea of his guilt for some shadowy wrong-doing in the past. When questioned, he is inconsistent in his references to his own life, assuming different identities as he tries to survive. To impress Meg he conjures up a life spent with varying success at the piano; to placate McCann he talks of a life begun and continued in a Maidenhead full of teashops and libraries, with 'a little private business', then, when really frightened, admits to years spent in Basingstoke during which he 'never stepped outside the door'; under interrogation he wildly talks of washing cups in a Lyons Corner House in London.

This shifting outline not only creates tension in the audience and conveys Stanley's anxiety, but is also an important aspect of Pinter's approach to character. In a speech made at the National Student Drama Festival in Bristol in 1962 (reprinted as the Introduction to *Pinter Plays: One*, London, Eyre Methuen, 1976), he said:

> The desire for verification is understandable, but cannot always be satisfied. There are no hard distinctions between what is real and what is unreal, nor between what is true and what is false. [. . .] A character on the stage who can present no convincing argument or information as to his past experiences, his present behaviour or his aspirations, nor give a comprehensive analysis of his motives, is as legitimate and as worthy of attention as one who, alarmingly, can do all these things. The more acute the experience, the less articulate its expression.

Quite apart from a character's wish to conceal his past or his inner life from others on the grounds that an open confession might incriminate him, there is the difficulty of being sure that what one remembers at any one moment is the truth, the whole truth, and nothing but the truth.

Pinteresque

What is 'Pinteresque'? The term is used to describe a style of play-writing where the dialogue appears to use the clichés and patterns of everyday conversation to express a darker sense of man's insecurity, aggressiveness, evasiveness, or hypocrisy. There is the repetition of phrases, at first merely trite, but becoming more telling with each utterance — perhaps revealing a character's private nightmare, or ambition, perhaps exploiting the absurdity of the phrase itself as a reflection of the emotional or intellectual poverty of the speaker. Conversations occur where characters use familiar phrases to escape the need to take real account of each other's demands, to ward off questions. This can be seen in the skirmish between Stanley and McCann at the beginning of Act II.

Yet Pinter denied that his plays were about failure of communication. 'I believe the contrary. I think that we communicate only too well, in our silence, in what is unsaid, and that what takes place is a continual evasion, desperate rearguard attempts to keep ourselves to ourselves.' (Introduction to *Pinter Plays: One*) This pressure to retreat from telling the whole truth, or from hearing the whole truth, makes sudden bursts of honesty, of betrayal or accusation, all the more startling. The pauses which Pinter deliberately calls for should never be seen merely as stopping places, empty spaces, but eloquent, revealing more about a character's anxieties or needs than words are allowed to.

There are moments when the dialogue ceases to echo the patterns of everyday speech; it gains the formality of classical drama. Greek tragedy employs the device of stichomythia — alternating one-line statements held together by a strong, under-lying rhythm. Goldberg and McCann sometimes shift into this highly organised form (page 83):

GOLDBERG: We'll make a man of you.
McCANN: And a woman.
GOLDBERG: You'll be re-orientated.
McCANN: You'll be rich.
GOLDBERG: You'll be adjusted.

McCANN: You'll be our pride and joy.
GOLDBERG: You'll be a mensch.
McCANN: You'll be a success.

This has the effect of heightening the impact of the scene, endowing the words with greater significance than naturalistic conversation could ever possess. As T.S. Eliot suggested in *A Dialogue on Dramatic Poetry*: 'The human soul, in intense emotion, strives to express itself in verse. [. . .] The tendency, at any rate, of prose drama is to emphasise the ephemeral and superficial; if we want to get at the permanent and universal we tend to express ourselves in verse.'

This form of heightened dialogue had been used a few years before Pinter wrote *The Birthday Party* by the Anglo-Irish playwright, poet and novelist, Samuel Beckett, whose play *Waiting for Godot* was greeted with confused hostility when it opened in London in 1955. The play has since proved to be highly influential and has gained considerable critical respectability. Two tramps, Vladimir and Estragon, try to while away the hours they must spend waiting for the mysterious Godot to come and give their lives meaning or purpose: they try to remember the past, they tell jokes, they argue, occasionally they are silent. Underlying their words is always an undercurrent of panic, of growing frustration, of near despair. The words themselves are modern, often funny, colloquial, shocking, but the sentence structure and rhythms are repeatedly ritualistic, like a litany or incantation.

VLADIMIR: He's not bad looking.
ESTRAGON: Would you say so?
VLADIMIR: A trifle effeminate.
ESTRAGON: Look at the slobber.
VLADIMIR: It's inevitable.
ESTRAGON: Look at the slaver.
VLADIMIR: Perhaps he's a half-wit.
ESTRAGON: A cretin.
VLADIMIR: It looks like a goitre.
ESTRAGON: It's not certain.
VLADIMIR: He's panting.
ESTRAGON: It's inevitable.

Compare this with Goldberg's and McCann's verbal assault on Stanley (page 82):

GOLDBERG: You look anaemic.

McCANN: Rheumatic.
GOLDBERG: Myopic.
McCANN: Epileptic.
GOLDBERG: You're on the verge.
McCANN: You're a dead duck.

Beckett's blustering, bullying, sanctimonious creation, Pozzo —
'Made in God's image!' — moves from facile sentiments — 'For
each one who begins to weep, somewhere else another stops' —
through violent hectoring of those who seem weaker than himself,
to moments of panic. This range of tone and idiom can also be seen
in Goldberg.

Unlike Beckett, whose characters inhabit a stark, unspecific
landscape, Pinter places his figures in recognisable surroundings,
stamped by the fashions of a particular period, leaving the quality
of the language and the enduring power of the images presented on
stage to endow the play with the universality of myth and the
seriousness of 'High Art'. This blend of the 'real', or recognisable,
and the 'surreal', mythic or at least strange, links his work to that
of the Czech writer Franz Kafka (1883—1924), another
acknowledged influence on Pinter. In Kafka's novel, *The Trial*, two
menacing strangers invade the bedroom of K. His efforts to beat a
dignified retreat are foiled, much as Stanley's efforts to leave are
blocked by McCann. When accused of unspecified crimes against
humanity, society and, possibly, the state, K tries to protest his
innocence, to placate his accusers, to make light of the danger:

> I cannot recall the slightest offence that might be charged
> against me. But that even is of minor importance, the real
> question is, who accuses me? What authority is conducting
> these proceedings? Are you officers of the law? None of you has
> a uniform, unless your suit — here he turned to Franz — is to be
> considered a uniform, but it's more like a tourist's outfit. I
> demand a clear answer to these questions, and I feel sure that
> after an explanation we shall be able to part from each other on
> the best of terms.

But, like Stanley after him, he fails to divert his pursuers from
their purpose and finally accepts his fate. K's executioners even
treat him with a curious kindness and courtesy:

> K shivered involuntarily, whereupon the man gave him a light
> reassuring pat on the back . . . The two of them laid K down on
> the ground, propped him against the boulder, and settled his

head upon it. But in spite of the pains they took and all the willingness K showed, his posture remained contorted and unnatural-looking.

This is disturbing in the same way as is Goldberg's and McCann's treatment of Stanley at the end of *The Birthday Party* (page 82): '*They begin to woo him, gently and with relish.*'

Pinter's work clearly stems from a well-established European tradition which includes writers such as Dostoevski and James Joyce, as well as Kafka and Beckett. When *The Birthday Party* was produced at the Lyric Theatre in Hammersmith in 1958, the critic of *The Manchester Guardian* was more aware of what the play shared with other dramatists than of what it contained that was new: 'If the author can forget Beckett, Ionesco and Simpson, he may do much better next time.'

Ionesco, a Rumanian playwright, and N.F. Simpson, an Englishman, are both classed as Absurdist writers; that is to say that their plays deliberately flouted traditional ideas of logic, both in terms of a plot where one event can be seen to proceed rationally from another through the interaction of consistent and credibly motivated characters, and in terms of language. Simpson's play, *A Resounding Tinkle*, was produced at the Royal Court Theatre in London in 1957, as one of the prize-winners in the *Observer* play competition. On a superficial level there are similarities with Pinter; at times Simpson employed a liturgical style, with a deliberate blending of mock seriousness and banality, involving sudden non-sequiturs and excursions into parody:

> PRAYER: Let us sing because round things roll:
> RESPONSE: And rejoice that it might have been otherwise.
> PRAYER: Let us praise God for woodlice, and for buildings sixty-nine feet three inches high:
> RESPONSE: For Adam Smith's *Wealth of Nations* published in 1776.
> PRAYER: For the fifth key from the left on the lower manual of the organ of the Church of the Ascension in the Piazza Vittorio Emanuele 11 in the town of Castelfidardo in Italy:
> RESPONSE: And for gnats.

The difference lies in the use to which these stylistic devices were put; with Simpson there is little sense of danger, of being threatened, challenged, or even involved. It is misleading, therefore, to assume, because N.F. Simpson and Harold Pinter both emerged during a renaissance of the British theatre in the late 1950s, sometimes referred to as 'The New Wave', and were associated with the Royal Court Theatre, that they both wrote the same kind of play. The drama critic of *The Manchester Guardian* might equally well have pointed out the echoes within *The Birthday Party* of the Winnie-the-Pooh stories written by A.A. Milne for his son, Christopher Robin, steeped in the attitudes and mannerisms of affluent Edwardian family life in the domesticated countryside of Kent.

> 'This party', said Christopher Robin, 'is a party because of what someone did, and we all know who it was, and it's his party, because of what he did, and I've got a present for him and here it is.'

> MEG: Well — it's very nice to be here tonight, in my house, and I want to propose a toast to Stanley, because it's his birthday, and he's lived here for a long while now, and he's my Stanley now. And I think he's a good boy, although sometimes he's bad. And he's the only Stanley I know, and I know him better than all the world, although he doesn't think so.

What is the play about? — Themes and interpretations

Not only did Pinter resist the 'verification' of a character's life history, he also resisted any attempt to provide interpretations of the play's action. 'To supply an explicit moral tag', he said in his speech to the students in 1962, 'to an evolving and compulsive dramatic image seems to be facile, impertinent and dishonest. Where this takes place it is not theatre but a crossword puzzle.' His interest and point of departure was always, he asserted, finding a couple of characters in a particular situation and listening to them.

> I never started a play from any kind of abstract idea or theory and never envisaged my own characters as messengers of death, doom, heaven or the milky way or, in other words, as allegorical representations of any particular force, whatever that may mean.

He argued that to interpret a character in symbolic terms was to emasculate him; Goldberg and McCann are less disturbing as elements in a dramatised debate or philosophical speculation than as the representation of two people with a job to do, and whose next assignment might well concern any member of the audience.

A symbol is too abstract to be menacing.

> When a character cannot be comfortably defined or understood in terms of the familiar, the tendency is to perch him on a symbolic shelf, out of harm's way. Once there, he can be talked about but need not be lived with.

Despite Pinter's caveat, however, *The Birthday Party* has been much interpreted. It has been seen as a social allegory: the Artist — Stanley, a musician — is forced to conform to the materialistic society which he has tried to reject. The values of this society are voiced by Goldberg and its pressures applied by McCann. They offer Stanley the benefits of belonging to a large corporation (page 82):

> GOLDBERG: From now on, we'll be the hub of your wheel.
> McCANN: We'll renew your season ticket.
> GOLDBERG: We'll take tuppence off your morning tea.
> McCANN: We'll give you a discount on all inflammable goods.
> GOLDBERG: We'll watch over you.

They offer assurance that the company benefits include treatment in case of breakdown or industrial disease (page 83):

> McCANN: We'll provide the skipping rope.
> GOLDBERG: The vest and pants.
> McCANN: The ointment.
> GOLDBERG: The hot poultice.
> McCANN: The fingerstall.
> GOLDBERG: The abdomen belt.

Stanley's 'submission' is seen as he dons the uniform of respectability, a dark suit and white collar.

Other critics, perhaps encouraged by Pinter's acknowledged debt to Samuel Beckett, see in *The Birthday Party* man's decay into death, life as a process of loss. Stanley loses first his sight, then his powers of speech and finally ceases to exist as a 'living' man; he is then taken away, dressed in funeral clothes, by two men in a large black hearse-like car. As Goldberg says to him (page 52): 'You're dead. You can't live, you can't think, you can't love. You're dead.'

It is also possible to see the play as demonstrating the individual's reluctance to leave the wet warmth of the womb and be born into a world which seems hostile. Meg mothers Stanley, feeds him, and shelters him from the outside. But life in the womb cannot continue indefinitely, nor can the foetus refuse to be born when his shelter is broken into and he is dragged out, unable to see clearly, unable to talk or to utter anything but inarticulate sounds of protest. It is his birth-day.

There is a view of *The Birthday Party* which is more political and historical, to do with a sense of the shared guilt implicit in any society which claims the individual's right to participate in decision-making, even if only through the occasional machinery of elections. Thus anyone living in a society which permits injustice or inhumanity may be called upon to pay the penalty for his acquiescence. Goldberg accuses: 'You betrayed our breed.' (p. 52). McCann asks: 'What about Ireland?' (p. 51). It is useless to protest, as Stanley does; 'It's a mistake.' (page 42).

It is important to remember, however, that these interpretations do not take account of the power of the play as a series of dramatic images which work partly on an intuitive, emotional, or even irrational level. The use of the drum and of darkness, the idea of a ritual, even of a kind of sacrifice, can be disturbing, even to modern, urban man.

Professor Konrad Lorenz in his book *On Aggression* (London, Methuen 1966) progressed from a study of aggression and appeasement patterns in animals, linked to the demands of territorial possession, sexual effectiveness and self-preservation, to a view of human behaviour as displaying essentially the same patterns, although sometimes in a more oblique or sophisticated form. The importance of territory, the manner of a man's response to intrusion from outside, the rivalry of males displaying before and competing for a sexually challenging female, have been commented on in a number of Pinter's plays, for example, *The Basement* and *The Homecoming*. The rituals of threat, appeasement, retreat, defence, and the shifting balance of mastery have the power to involve an audience because they appeal to deeply-rooted responses which are universal and have little to do with education or an enthusiasm for dramatic theory or philosophical debate.

Goldberg and McCann invade Stanley's territory; he displays fear, attempts appeasement, struggles desperately, surrenders. The development of the relationship between these three characters in *The Birthday Party* seems to follow patterns described by Lorenz:

The first step from injury-inflicting to the ritualised fight consists of the lengthening of the periods between the single,

> gradually increasing threatening movements and the final
> assault. [. . .] The longer they last, the more ritualised the
> threatening movements become, and this leads to mimic
> exaggeration, rhythmical repetition. (*On Aggression*, pp. 96-97)

The interrogation of Stanley, from 'Mr. Webber, sit down' to the
moment when Stanley kicks Goldberg and then he and McCann
circle each other, chairs raised, presents just such a ritualised
conflict. Stanley's final submission, his passivity once he realises
that escape is impossible, is similar to the behaviour that Lorenz
observed among rats:

> Only rarely does one see an animal in such desperation and
> panic, so conscious of a terrible death, as a rat which is about
> to be slain by rats. It ceases to defend itself. (Ibid., p. 139)

This is not to suggest that Pinter deliberately set out to dramatise
Darwin or Lorenz or Freud. In his speech to the students at Bristol
in 1962, he emphasised that he began his plays in what he called
'quite a simple manner'. He had usually 'found a couple of
characters in a particular context, thrown them together and
listened to what they said'. Thus, no matter how richly endowed
the early plays — including *The Birthday Party* — may be with
symbols, or literary allusions, or philosophical arguments, they
are firmly rooted in real life, suggested by specific experiences
which were then developed and shaped into dramatic form by
Pinter.

> The function of selection and arrangement is mine. I do all the
> donkeywork, in fact, and I think I can say I pay meticulous
> attention to the shape of things, from the shape of a sentence
> to the overall structure of the play. This shaping, to put it
> mildly, is of the first importance. (Introduction to *Pinter Plays:
> One*)

The Room, for example, was suggested by the moment during a
party in London when Pinter opened a door into a small room and
discovered two men sitting at a table: one, a small man, was talking
vivaciously while slicing and buttering bread to feed the huge,
silent lorry driver next to him. The image, Pinter says, stayed with
him. Similarly, *The Birthday Party* was suggested by the grotesque
surroundings he found himself in while an actor in provincial
repertory theatre. In an interview given in 1966 for *The Paris
Review* , Pinter described the circumstances which had given him

the first ideas for the play:

> *The Birthday Party* had also been in my mind for a long time.
> It was sparked off from a very distinct situation in digs when I
> was on tour. In fact the other day a friend of mine gave me a
> letter I wrote him in nineteen-fifty something, Christ knows
> when it was. This is what it says. 'I have filthy insane digs, a
> great bulging scrag of a woman with breasts rolling at her belly,
> an obscene household, cats, dogs, filth, tea-strainers, mess.'
> [. . .] Now the thing about this is *that* was *The Birthday Party*
> — I was in those digs, and this woman was Meg in the play, and
> there was a fellow staying there in Eastbourne, on the coast.
> The whole thing remained with me, and three years later I
> wrote the play.

Pinter supplemented this description in an interview for the
Listener, 6 November 1969:

> I found digs in which a man had to share a room with a man in
> a kind of attic . . . At the end of the week I said to this fellow,
> who turned out to have been a concert pianist on the pier, 'Why
> do you stay here?' and he said 'There's nowhere else to go.' I
> left with that ringing in my ears. Then about a year or so later
> I started to write *The Birthday Party*, but it has no relation to
> that original thing, that situation in Eastbourne, other than that
> there were two people who got me on to the first page.

Suggestions for further reading

Collections of Pinter's writings

All Pinter's plays up to 1981 (except for *The Hothouse*, which is available only in a separate edition) have been collected in four paperback volumes: *Plays: One, Plays: Two, Plays: Three,* and *Plays: Four* (Eyre Methuen: Master Playwrights series).

Five Screenplays (Eyre Methuen: paperback) contains *The Servant, The Pumpkin Eater, The Quiller Memorandum, Accident* and *The Go-Between. Three Screenplays* (Eyre Methuen: paperback), containing *The Last Tycoon, Langrishe, Go Down* and *The French Lieutenant's Woman* is scheduled for publication in 1982. *A la Recherche du Temps Perdu* is published separately (Eyre Methuen: paperback).

Poems and Prose 1949–1977 (Eyre Methuen: paperback) is a selection of Pinter's non-dramatic writings.

General critical studies (all with sections on *The Birthday Party*)

Martin Esslin, *Pinter: A study of His Plays* (Eyre Methuen: Modern Theatre Profiles). Now in its third, revised and expanded edition, 1977.

Ronald Hayman, *Harold Pinter* (Heinemann Education Books, 1968: Contemporary Playwrights series).

Arnold P. Hinchcliffe, *Harold Pinter* (Twayne, New York, 1967: Twayne's English Authors series).

Simon Trussler, *The Plays of Harold Pinter: An Assessment* (Gollancz, 1973).

Martin Esslin, *The Theatre of the Absurd* (Penguin, revised 1980). Sets Pinter in a wider, European context.

John Russell Taylor, *Anger and After: A Guide to the New British Drama* (Eyre Methuen, revised 1969). Good for the background to the theatre of the late fifties and early sixties.

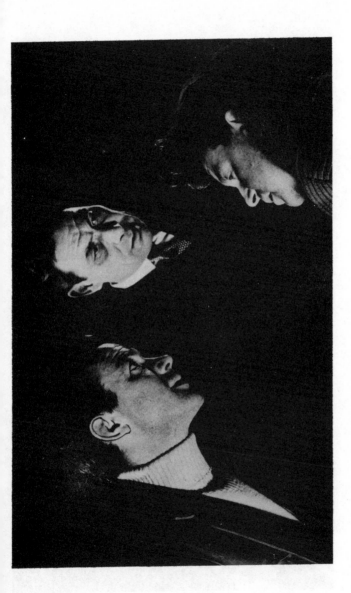

McCann, Goldberg, Stanley: original stage production, London, 1958

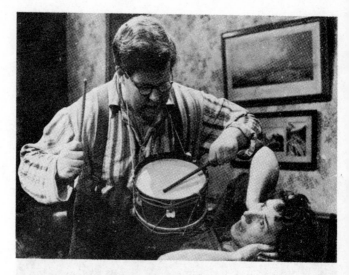

Above: Stanley, Meg: British television, 1960 *Below*: Meg, Stanley:
Royal Shakespeare Company, London, 1964

McCann: Cheltenham

Above: Goldberg, Stanley, McCann: Göteborg, Sweden, 1964 *Below*: McCann, Stanley, Goldberg: EMI film, 1968

Goldberg, Meg: Montreal, Canada, 1970

Above: McCann, Stanley, Goldberg; *Below*: Meg, McCann, Goldberg, Lulu, Stanley (seated): both from Tel-Aviv, Israel

The Birthday Party

THE BIRTHDAY PARTY was first presented by Michael Codron and David Hall at the Arts Theatre, Cambridge, on 28 April, 1958, and subsequently at the Lyric Opera House, Hammersmith, with the following cast:

PETEY, *a man in his sixties*	Willoughby Gray
MEG, *a woman in her sixties*	Beatrix Lehmann
STANLEY, *a man in his late thirties*	Richard Pearson
LULU, *a girl in her twenties*	Wendy Hutchinson
GOLDBERG, *a man in his fifties*	John Slater
MCCANN, *a man of thirty*	John Stratton

Directed by Peter Wood

ACT I A morning in summer

ACT II Evening of the same day

ACT III The next morning

THE BIRTHDAY PARTY was revived by the Royal Shakespeare Company at the Aldwych Theatre, London, on June 18th, 1964 with the following cast:

PETEY	Newton Blick
MEG	Doris Hare
STANLEY	Bryan Pringle
LULU	Janet Suzman
GOLDBERG	Brewster Mason
MCCANN	Patrick Magee

Directed by Harold Pinter

Act One

The living-room of a house in a seaside town. A door leading to the hall down left. Back door and small window up left. Kitchen hatch, centre back. Kitchen door up right. Table and chairs, centre.

PETEY enters from the door on the left with a paper and sits at the table. He begins to read. MEG'S voice comes through the kitchen hatch.

MEG. Is that you, Petey?

    Pause.

Petey, is that you?

    Pause.

Petey?

PETEY. What?

MEG. Is that you?

PETEY. Yes, it's me.

MEG. What? (*Her face appears at the hatch.*) Are you back?

PETEY. Yes.

MEG. I've got your cornflakes ready. (*She disappears and re-appears.*) Here's your cornflakes.

    He rises and takes the plate from her, sits at the table, props up the paper and begins to eat. MEG enters by the kitchen door.

Are they nice?

PETEY. Very nice.

MEG. I thought they'd be nice. (*She sits at the table.*) You got your paper?

PETEY. Yes.

MEG. Is it good?

PETEY. Not bad.

MEG. What does it say?

PETEY. Nothing much.

MEG. You read me out some nice bits yesterday.

PETEY. Yes, well, I haven't finished this one yet.

MEG. Will you tell me when you come to something good?

PETEY. Yes.

> *Pause.*

MEG. Have you been working hard this morning?

PETEY. No. Just stacked a few of the old chairs. Cleaned up a bit.

MEG. Is it nice out?

PETEY. Very nice.

> *Pause.*

MEG. Is Stanley up yet?

PETEY. I don't know. Is he?

MEG. I don't know. I haven't seen him down yet.

PETEY. Well then, he can't be up.

MEG. Haven't you seen him down?

PETEY. I've only just come in.

MEG. He must be still asleep.

> *She looks round the room, stands, goes to the sideboard and takes a pair of socks from a drawer, collects wool and a needle and goes back to the table.*

What time did you go out this morning, Petey?

PETEY. Same time as usual.

MEG. Was it dark?

PETEY. No, it was light.

MEG (*beginning to darn*). But sometimes you go out in the morning and it's dark.

PETEY. That's in the winter.

MEG. Oh, in winter.

PETEY. Yes, it gets light later in winter.
MEG. Oh.

> *Pause.*

What are you reading?
PETEY. Someone's just had a baby.
MEG. Oh, they haven't! Who?
PETEY. Some girl.
MEG. Who, Petey, who?
PETEY. I don't think you'd know her.
MEG. What's her name?
PETEY. Lady Mary Splatt.
MEG. I don't know her.
PETEY. No.
MEG. What is it?
PETEY (*studying the paper*). Er—a girl.
MEG. Not a boy?
PETEY. No.
MEG. Oh, what a shame. I'd be sorry. I'd much rather have a
little boy.
PETEY. A little girl's all right.
MEG. I'd much rather have a little boy.

> *Pause.*

PETEY. I've finished my cornflakes.
MEG. Were they nice?
PETEY. Very nice.
MEG. I've got something else for you.
PETEY. Good.

> *She rises, takes his plate and exits into the kitchen. She then
> appears at the hatch with two pieces of fried bread on a plate.*

MEG. Here you are, Petey.

> *He rises, collects the plate, looks at it, sits at the table.* MEG
> *re-enters.*

Is it nice?

PETEY. I haven't tasted it yet.

MEG. I bet you don't know what it is.

PETEY. Yes, I do.

MEG. What is it, then?

PETEY. Fried bread.

MEG. That's right.

> *He begins to eat.*
> *She watches him eat.*

PETEY. Very nice.

MEG. I knew it was.

PETEY (*turning to her*). Oh, Meg, two men came up to me on the beach last night.

MEG. Two men?

PETEY. Yes. They wanted to know if we could put them up for a couple of nights.

MEG. Put them up? Here?

PETEY. Yes.

MEG. How many men?

PETEY. Two.

MEG. What did you say?

PETEY. Well, I said I didn't know. So they said they'd come round to find out.

MEG. Are they coming?

PETEY. Well, they said they would.

MEG. Had they heard about us, Petey?

PETEY. They must have done.

MEG. Yes, they must have done. They must have heard this was a very good boarding house. It is. This house is on the list.

PETEY. It is.

MEG. I know it is.

PETEY. They might turn up today. Can you do it?

MEG. Oh, I've got that lovely room they can have.

PETEY. You've got a room ready?

MEG. I've got the room with the armchair all ready for visitors.

PETEY. You're sure?

MEG. Yes, that'll be all right then, if they come today.

PETEY. Good.

She takes the socks etc. back to the sideboard drawer.

MEG. I'm going to wake that boy.

PETEY. There's a new show coming to the Palace.

MEG. On the pier?

PETEY. No. The Palace, in the town.

MEG. Stanley could have been in it, if it was on the pier.

PETEY. This is a straight show.

MEG. What do you mean?

PETEY. No dancing or singing.

MEG. What do they do then?

PETEY. They just talk.

Pause.

MEG. Oh.

PETEY. You like a song eh, Meg?

MEG. I like listening to the piano. I used to like watching Stanley play the piano. Of course, he didn't sing. (*Looking at the door.*) I'm going to call that boy.

PETEY. Didn't you take him up his cup of tea?

MEG. I always take him up his cup of tea. But that was a long time ago.

PETEY. Did he drink it?

MEG. I made him. I stood there till he did. I'm going to call him. (*She goes to the door.*) Stan! Stanny! (*She listens.*) Stan! I'm coming up to fetch you if you don't come down! I'm coming up! I'm going to count three! One! Two! Three! I'm coming to get you! (*She exits and goes upstairs. In a moment, shouts from* STANLEY, *wild laughter from* MEG. PETEY *takes his plate to the hatch. Shouts. Laughter.*

PETEY *sits at the table. Silence. She returns.*) He's coming
down. (*She is panting and arranges her hair.*) I told him if he
didn't hurry up he'd get no breakfast.

PETEY. That did it, eh?

MEG. I'll get his cornflakes.

    MEG *exits to the kitchen.* PETEY *reads the paper.* STANLEY
    *enters. He is unshaven, in his pyjama jacket and wears
    glasses. He sits at the table.*

PETEY. Morning, Stanley.

STANLEY. Morning.

    Silence. MEG *enters with the bowl of cornflakes, which she
    sets on the table.*

MEG. So he's come down at last, has he? He's come down at
last for his breakfast. But he doesn't deserve any, does he,
Petey? (STANLEY *stares at the cornflakes.*) Did you sleep
well?

STANLEY. I didn't sleep at all.

MEG. You didn't sleep at all? Did you hear that, Petey? Too
tired to eat your breakfast, I suppose? Now you eat up those
cornflakes like a good boy. Go on.

    He begins to eat.

STANLEY. What's it like out today?

PETEY. Very nice.

STANLEY. Warm?

PETEY. Well, there's a good breeze blowing.

STANLEY. Cold?

PETEY. No, no, I wouldn't say it was cold.

MEG. What are the cornflakes like, Stan?

STANLEY. Horrible.

MEG. Those flakes? Those lovely flakes? You're a liar, a little
liar. They're refreshing. It says so. For people when they get
up late.

STANLEY. The milk's off.

MEG. It's not. Petey ate his, didn't you, Petey?

PETEY. That's right.

MEG. There you are then.

STANLEY. All right, I'll go on to the second course.

MEG. He hasn't finished the first course and he wants to go on to the second course!

STANLEY. I feel like something cooked.

MEG. Well, I'm not going to give it to you.

PETEY. Give it to him.

MEG (*sitting at the table, right*). I'm not going to.

> *Pause.*

STANLEY. No breakfast.

> *Pause.*

All night long I've been dreaming about this breakfast.

MEG. I thought you said you didn't sleep.

STANLEY. Day-dreaming. All night long. And now she won't give me any. Not even a crust of bread on the table.

> *Pause.*

Well, I can see I'll have to go down to one of those smart hotels on the front.

MEG (*rising quickly*). You won't get a better breakfast there than here.

> *She exits to the kitchen.* STANLEY *yawns broadly.* MEG *appears at the hatch with a plate.*

Here you are. You'll like this.

> PETEY *rises, collects the plate, brings it to the table, puts it in front of* STANLEY, *and sits.*

STANLEY. What's this?

PETEY. Fried bread.

MEG (*entering*). Well, I bet you don't know what it is.

STANLEY. Oh yes I do.

MEG. What?

STANLEY. Fried bread.

MEG. He knew.

STANLEY. What a wonderful surprise.

MEG. You didn't expect that, did you?

STANLEY. I bloody well didn't.

PETEY (*rising*). Well, I'm off.

MEG. You going back to work?

PETEY. Yes.

MEG. Your tea! You haven't had your tea!

PETEY. That's all right. No time now.

MEG. I've got it made inside.

PETEY. No, never mind. See you later. Ta-ta, Stan.

STANLEY. Ta-ta.

   PETEY *exits, left.*

   Tch, tch, tch, tch.

MEG (*defensively*). What do you mean?

STANLEY. You're a bad wife.

MEG. I'm not. Who said I am?

STANLEY. Not to make your husband a cup of tea. Terrible.

MEG. He knows I'm not a bad wife.

STANLEY. Giving him sour milk instead.

MEG. It wasn't sour.

STANLEY. Disgraceful.

MEG. You mind your own business, anyway. (STANLEY *eats.*)
   You won't find many better wives than me, I can tell you. I
   keep a very nice house and I keep it clean.

STANLEY. Whoo!

MEG. Yes! And this house is very well known, for a very good
   boarding house for visitors.

STANLEY. Visitors? Do you know how many visitors you've
   had since I've been here?

MEG. How many?

STANLEY. One.

MEG. Who?

STANLEY. Me! I'm your visitor.

MEG. You're a liar. This house is on the list.

STANLEY. I bet it is.

MEG. I know it is.

He pushes his plate away and picks up the paper.

  Was it nice?

STANLEY. What?

MEG. The fried bread.

STANLEY. Succulent.

MEG. You shouldn't say that word.

STANLEY. What word?

MEG. That word you said.

STANLEY. What, succulent—?

MEG. Don't say it!

STANLEY. What's the matter with it?

MEG. You shouldn't say that word to a married woman.

STANLEY. Is that a fact?

MEG. Yes.

STANLEY. Well, I never knew that.

MEG. Well, it's true.

STANLEY. Who told you that?

MEG. Never you mind.

STANLEY. Well, if I can't say it to a married woman who can I
  say it to?

MEG. You're bad.

STANLEY. What about some tea?

MEG. Do you want some tea? (STANLEY *reads the paper.*) Say
  please.

STANLEY. Please.

MEG. Say sorry first.

STANLEY. Sorry first.

MEG. No. Just sorry.

STANLEY. Just sorry!

MEG. You deserve the strap.

STANLEY. Don't do that!

> *She takes his plate and ruffles his hair as she passes.* STANLEY *exclaims and throws her arm away. She goes into the kitchen. He rubs his eyes under his glasses and picks up the paper. She enters.*

I brought the pot in.

STANLEY (*absently*). I don't know what I'd do without you.

MEG. You don't deserve it though.

STANLEY. Why not?

MEG (*pouring the tea, coyly*). Go on. Calling me that.

STANLEY. How long has that tea been in the pot?

MEG. It's good tea. Good strong tea.

STANLEY. This isn't tea. It's gravy!

MEG. It's not.

STANLEY. Get out of it. You succulent old washing bag.

MEG. I am not! And it isn't your place to tell me if I am!

STANLEY. And it isn't your place to come into a man's bed-room and—wake him up.

MEG. Stanny! Don't you like your cup of tea of a morning—the one I bring you?

STANLEY. I can't drink this muck. Didn't anyone ever tell you to warm the pot, at least?

MEG. That's good strong tea, that's all.

STANLEY (*putting his head in his hands*). Oh God, I'm tired.

> *Silence.* MEG *goes to the sideboard, collects a duster, and vaguely dusts the room, watching him. She comes to the table and dusts it.*

Not the bloody table!

> *Pause.*

MEG. Stan?

STANLEY. What?

MEG (*shyly*). Am I really succulent?

STANLEY. Oh, you are. I'd rather have you than a cold in the
  nose any day.

MEG. You're just saying that.

STANLEY (*violently*). Look, why don't you get this place
  cleared up! It's a pigsty. And another thing, what about
  my room? It needs sweeping. It needs papering. I need a
  new room!

MEG (*sensual, stroking his arm*). Oh, Stan, that's a lovely room.
  I've had some lovely afternoons in that room.

> *He recoils from her hand in disgust, stands and exits quickly
> by the door on the left. She collects his cup and the teapot
> and takes them to the hatch shelf. The street door slams.*
> STANLEY *returns.*

MEG. Is the sun shining? (*He crosses to the window, takes a
  cigarette and matches from his pyjama jacket, and lights his
  cigarette.*) What are you smoking?

STANLEY. A cigarette.

MEG. Are you going to give me one?

STANLEY. No.

MEG. I like cigarettes. (*He stands at the window, smoking. She
  crosses behind him and tickles the back of his neck.*) Tickle,
  tickle.

STANLEY (*pushing her*). Get away from me.

MEG. Are you going out?

STANLEY. Not with you.

MEG. But I'm going shopping in a minute.

STANLEY. Go.

MEG. You'll be lonely, all by yourself.

STANLEY. Will I?

MEG. Without your old Meg. I've got to get things in for the
  two gentlemen.

A pause. STANLEY *slowly raises his head. He speaks without turning.*

STANLEY. What two gentlemen?

MEG. I'm expecting visitors.

He turns.

STANLEY. What?

MEG. You didn't know that, did you?

STANLEY. What are you talking about?

MEG. Two gentlemen asked Petey if they could come and stay for a couple of nights. I'm expecting them. (*She picks up the duster and begins to wipe the cloth on the table.*)

STANLEY. I don't believe it.

MEG. It's true.

STANLEY (*moving to her*). You're saying it on purpose.

MEG. Petey told me this morning.

STANLEY (*grinding his cigarette*). When was this? When did he see them?

MEG. Last night.

STANLEY. Who are they?

MEG. I don't know.

STANLEY. Didn't he tell you their names?

MEG. No.

STANLEY (*pacing the room*). Here? They wanted to come here?

MEG. Yes, they did. (*She takes the curlers out of her hair.*)

STANLEY. Why?

MEG. This house is on the list.

STANLEY. But who are they?

MEG. You'll see when they come.

STANLEY (*decisively*). They won't come.

MEG. Why not?

STANLEY (*quickly*). I tell you they won't come. Why didn't they come last night, if they were coming?

MEG. Perhaps they couldn't find the place in the dark. It's not easy to find in the dark.

STANLEY. They won't come. Someone's taking the Michael.
Forget all about it. It's a false alarm. A false alarm. (*He sits
at the table.*) Where's my tea?

MEG. I took it away. You didn't want it.

STANLEY. What do you mean, you took it away?

MEG. I took it away.

STANLEY. What did you take it away for?

MEG. You didn't want it!

STANLEY. Who said I didn't want it?

MEG. You did!

STANLEY. Who gave you the right to take away my tea?

MEG. You wouldn't drink it.

> STANLEY *stares at her.*

STANLEY (*quietly*). Who do you think you're talking to?

MEG (*uncertainly*). What?

STANLEY. Come here.

MEG. What do you mean?

STANLEY. Come over here.

MEG. No.

STANLEY. I want to ask you something. (MEG *fidgets ner-
vously. She does not go to him.*) Come on. (*Pause.*) All right.
I can ask it from here just as well. (*Deliberately.*) Tell me,
Mrs Boles, when you address yourself to me, do you ever
ask yourself who exactly you are talking to? Eh?

> *Silence. He groans, his trunk falls forward, his head falls into
> his hands.*

MEG (*in a small voice*). Didn't you enjoy your breakfast, Stan?
(*She approaches the table.*) Stan? When are you going to
play the piano again? (STANLEY *grunts.*) Like you used to?
(STANLEY *grunts.*) I used to like watching you play the
piano. When are you going to play it again?

STANLEY. I can't, can I?

MEG. Why not?

STANLEY. I haven't got a piano, have I?

MEG. No, I meant like when you were working. That piano.

STANLEY. Go and do your shopping.

MEG. But you wouldn't have to go away if you got a job, would you? You could play the piano on the pier.

He looks at her, then speaks airily.

STANLEY. I've . . . er . . . I've been offered a job, as a matter of fact.

MEG. What?

STANLEY. Yes. I'm considering a job at the moment.

MEG. You're not.

STANLEY. A good one, too. A night club. In Berlin.

MEG. Berlin?

STANLEY. Berlin. A night club. Playing the piano. A fabulous salary. And all found.

MEG. How long for?

STANLEY. We don't stay in Berlin. Then we go to Athens.

MEG. How long for?

STANLEY. Yes. Then we pay a flying visit to . . . er . . . whatsisname. . . .

MEG. Where?

STANLEY. Constantinople. Zagreb. Vladivostock. It's a round the world tour.

MEG (*sitting at the table*). Have you played the piano in those places before?

STANLEY. Played the piano? I've played the piano all over the world. All over the country. (*Pause.*) I once gave a concert.

MEG. A concert?

STANLEY (*reflectively*). Yes. It was a good one, too. They were all there that night. Every single one of them. It was a great success. Yes. A concert. At Lower Edmonton.

MEG. What did you wear?

STANLEY (*to himself*). I had a unique touch. Absolutely unique. They came up to me. They came up to me and said they were grateful. Champagne we had that night, the lot. (*Pause.*) My father nearly came down to hear me. Well, I dropped him a card anyway. But I don't think he could make it. No, I—I lost the address, that was it. (*Pause.*) Yes. Lower Edmonton. Then after that, you know what they did? They carved me up. Carved me up. It was all arranged, it was all worked out. My next concert. Somewhere else it was. In winter. I went down there to play. Then, when I got there, the hall was closed, the place was shuttered up, not even a caretaker. They'd locked it up. (*Takes off his glasses and wipes them on his pyjama jacket.*) A fast one. They pulled a fast one. I'd like to know who was responsible for that. (*Bitterly.*) All right, Jack, I can take a tip. They want me to crawl down on my bended knees. Well I can take a tip . . . any day of the week. (*He replaces his glasses, then looks at* MEG.) Look at her. You're just an old piece of rock cake, aren't you? (*He rises and leans across the table to her.*) That's what you are, aren't you?

MEG. Don't you go away again, Stan. You stay here. You'll be better off. You stay with your old Meg. (*He groans and lies across the table.*) Aren't you feeling well this morning, Stan. Did you pay a visit this morning?

He stiffens, then lifts himself slowly, turns to face her and speaks lightly, casually.

STANLEY. Meg. Do you know what?
MEG. What?
STANLEY. Have you heard the latest?
MEG. No.
STANLEY. I'll bet you have.
MEG. I haven't.
STANLEY. Shall I tell you?
MEG. What latest?
STANLEY. You haven't heard it?
MEG. No.

STANLEY (*advancing*). They're coming today.

MEG. Who?

STANLEY. They're coming in a van.

MEG. Who?

STANLEY. And do you know what they've got in that van?

MEG. What?

STANLEY. They've got a wheelbarrow in that van.

MEG (*breathlessly*). They haven't.

STANLEY. Oh yes they have.

MEG. You're a liar.

STANLEY (*advancing upon her*). A big wheelbarrow. And when the van stops they wheel it out, and they wheel it up the garden path, and then they knock at the front door.

MEG. They don't.

STANLEY. They're looking for someone.

MEG. They're not.

STANLEY. They're looking for someone. A certain person.

MEG (*hoarsely*). No, they're not!

STANLEY. Shall I tell you who they're looking for?

MEG. No!

STANLEY. You don't want me to tell you?

MEG. You're a liar!

> *A sudden knock on the front door.* LULU'S *voice: Ooh-ooh!* MEG *edges past* STANLEY *and collects her shopping bag.* MEG *goes out.* STANLEY *sidles to the door and listens.*

VOICE (*through letter box*). Hullo, Mrs Boles . . .

MEG. Oh, has it come?

VOICE. Yes, it's just come.

MEG. What, is that it?

VOICE. Yes. I thought I'd bring it round.

MEG. Is it nice?

VOICE. Very nice. What shall I do with it?

MEG. Well, I don't . . . (*Whispers.*)

VOICE. No, of course not . . .(*Whispers.*)

MEG. All right, but . . . (*Whispers.*)
VOICE. I won't . . . (*Whispers.*) Ta-ta, Mrs Boles.

STANLEY *quickly sits at the table. Enter* LULU.

LULU. Oh, hullo.
STANLEY. Ay-ay.
LULU. I just want to leave this in here.
STANLEY. Do. (LULU *crosses to the sideboard and puts a solid, round parcel upon it.*) That's a bulky object.
LULU. You're not to touch it.
STANLEY. Why would I want to touch it?
LULU. Well, you're not to, anyway.

LULU *walks upstage.*

LULU. Why don't you open the door? It's all stuffy in here.

She opens the back door.

STANLEY (*rising*): Stuffy? I disinfected the place this morning.
LULU (*at the door*). Oh, that's better.
STANLEY. I think it's going to rain to-day. What do you think?
LULU. I hope so. You could do with it.
STANLEY. Me! I was in the sea at half past six.
LULU. Were you?
STANLEY. I went right out to the headland and back before breakfast. Don't you believe me!

She sits, takes out a compact and powders her nose.

LULU (*offering him the compact*). Do you want to have a look at your face? (STANLEY *withdraws from the table.*) You could do with a shave, do you know that? (STANLEY *sits, right at the table.*) Don't you ever go out? (*He does not answer.*) I mean, what do you do, just sit around the house like this all day long? (*Pause.*) Hasn't Mrs Boles got enough to do without having you under her feet all day long?

STANLEY. I always stand on the table when she sweeps the floor.

LULU. Why don't you have a wash? You look terrible.

STANLEY. A wash wouldn't make any difference.

LULU (*rising*). Come out and get a bit of air. You depress me, looking like that.

STANLEY. Air? Oh, I don't know about that.

LULU. It's lovely out. And I've got a few sandwiches.

STANLEY. What sort of sandwiches?

LULU. Cheese.

STANLEY. I'm a big eater, you know.

LULU. That's all right. I'm not hungry.

STANLEY (*abruptly*). How would you like to go away with me?

LULU. Where.

STANLEY. Nowhere. Still, we could go.

LULU. But where could we go?

STANLEY. Nowhere. There's nowhere to go. So we could just go. It wouldn't matter.

LULU. We might as well stay here.

STANLEY. No. It's no good here.

LULU. Well, where else is there?

STANLEY. Nowhere.

LULU. Well, that's a charming proposal. (*He gets up.*) Do you have to wear those glasses?

STANLEY. Yes.

LULU. So you're not coming out for a walk?

STANLEY. I can't at the moment.

LULU. You're a bit of a washout, aren't you?

She exits, left. STANLEY *stands. He then goes to the mirror and looks in it. He goes into the kitchen, takes off his glasses and begins to wash his face. A pause. Enter, by the back door,* GOLDBERG *and* MCCANN. MCCANN *carries two suitcases,* GOLDBERG *a briefcase. They halt inside the door, then walk downstage.* STANLEY, *wiping his face, glimpses their backs through the hatch.* GOLDBERG *and* MCCANN *look round the room.* STANLEY *slips on his glasses, sidles through the kitchen door and out of the back door.*

MCCANN. Is this it?

GOLDBERG. This is it.

MCCANN. Are you sure?

GOLDBERG. Sure I'm sure.

Pause.

MCCANN. What now?

GOLDBERG. Don't worry yourself, McCann. Take a seat.

MCCANN. What about you?

GOLDBERG. What about me?

MCCANN. Are you going to take a seat?

GOLDBERG. We'll both take a seat. (MCCANN *puts down the suitcase and sits at the table, left.*) Sit back, McCann. Relax. What's the matter with you? I bring you down for a few days to the seaside. Take a holiday. Do yourself a favour. Learn to relax, McCann, or you'll never get anywhere.

MCCANN. Ah sure, I do try, Nat.

GOLDBERG (*sitting at the table, right*). The secret is breathing. Take my tip. It's a well-known fact. Breathe in, breathe out, take a chance, let yourself go, what can you lose? Look at me. When I was an apprentice yet, McCann, every second Friday of the month my Uncle Barney used to take me to the seaside, regular as clockwork. Brighton, Canvey Island, Rottingdean—Uncle Barney wasn't particular. After lunch on Shabbuss we'd go and sit in a couple of deck chairs—you know, the ones with canopies—we'd have a little paddle, we'd watch the tide coming in, going out, the sun coming down—golden days, believe me, McCann. (*Reminiscent.*) Uncle Barney. Of course, he was an impeccable dresser. One of the old school. He had a house just outside Basingstoke at the time. Respected by the whole community.

Culture? Don't talk to me about culture. He was an all-round man, what do you mean? He was a cosmopolitan.

MCCANN. Hey, Nat. . . .

GOLDBERG (*reflectively*). Yes. One of the old school.

MCCANN. Nat. How do we know this is the right house?

GOLDBERG. What?

MCCANN. How do we know this is the right house?

GOLDBERG. What makes you think it's the wrong house?

MCCANN. I didn't see a number on the gate.

GOLDBERG. I wasn't looking for a number.

MCCANN. No?

GOLDBERG (*settling in the armchair*). You know one thing Uncle Barney taught me? Uncle Barney taught me that the word of a gentleman is enough. That's why, when I had to go away on business I never carried any money. One of my sons used to come with me. He used to carry a few coppers. For a paper, perhaps, to see how the M.C.C. was getting on overseas. Otherwise my name was good. Besides, I was a very busy man.

MCCANN. What about this, Nat? Isn't it about time someone came in?

GOLDBERG. McCann, what are you so nervous about? Pull yourself together. Everywhere you go these days it's like a funeral.

MCCANN. That's true.

GOLDBERG. True? Of course it's true. It's more than true. It's a fact.

MCCANN. You may be right.

GOLDBERG. What is it, McCann? You don't trust me like you did in the old days?

MCCANN. Sure I trust you, Nat.

GOLDBERG. But why is it that before you do a job you're all over the place, and when you're doing the job you're as cool as a whistle?

MCCANN. I don't know, Nat. I'm just all right once I know what I'm doing. When I know what I'm doing, I'm all right.

GOLDBERG. Well, you do it very well.

MCCANN. Thank you, Nat.

GOLDBERG. You know what I said when this job came up. I mean naturally they approached me to take care of it. And you know who I asked for?

MCCANN. Who?

GOLDBERG. You.

MCCANN. That was very good of you, Nat.

GOLDBERG. No, it was nothing. You're a capable man, McCann.

MCCANN. That's a great compliment, Nat, coming from a man in your position.

GOLDBERG. Well, I've got a position, I won't deny it.

MCCANN. You certainly have.

GOLDBERG. I would never deny that I had a position.

MCCANN. And what a position!

GOLDBERG. It's not a thing I would deny.

MCCANN. Yes, it's true, you've done a lot for me. I appreciate it.

GOLDBERG. Say no more.

MCCANN. You've always been a true Christian.

GOLDBERG. In a way.

MCCANN. No, I just thought I'd tell you that I appreciate it.

GOLDBERG. It's unnecessary to recapitulate.

MCCANN. You're right there.

GOLDBERG. Quite unnecessary.

Pause. MCCANN *leans forward.*

MCCANN. Hey Nat, just one thing. . . .

GOLDBERG. What now?

MCCANN. This job—no, listen—this job, is it going to be like anything we've ever done before?

GOLDBERG. Tch, tch, tch.

MCCANN. No, just tell me that. Just that, and I won't ask any more.

> GOLDBERG *sighs, stands, goes behind the table, ponders, looks at* MCCANN, *and then speaks in a quiet, fluent, official tone.*

GOLDBERG. The main issue is a singular issue and quite distinct from your previous work. Certain elements, however, might well approximate in points of procedure to some of your other activities. All is dependent on the attitude of our subject. At all events, McCann, I can assure you that the assignment will be carried out and the mission accomplished with no excessive aggravation to you or myself. Satisfied?

MCCANN. Sure. Thank you, Nat.

> MEG *enters, left.*

GOLDBERG. Ah, Mrs Boles?

MEG. Yes?

GOLDBERG. We spoke to your husband last night. Perhaps he mentioned us? We heard that you kindly let rooms for gentlemen. So I brought my friend along with me. We were after a nice place, you understand. So we came to you. I'm Mr Goldberg and this is Mr McCann.

MEG. Very pleased to meet you.

> *They shake hands.*

GOLDBERG. We're pleased to meet you, too.

MEG. That's very nice.

GOLDBERG. You're right. How often do you meet someone it's a pleasure to meet?

MCCANN. Never.

GOLDBERG. But today it's different. How are you keeping, Mrs Boles?

MEG. Oh, very well, thank you.

GOLDBERG. Yes? Really?

MEG. Oh yes, really.

GOLDBERG. I'm glad.

    GOLDBERG *sits at the table, right.*

GOLDBERG. Well, so what do you say? You can manage to put us up, eh, Mrs Boles?

MEG. Well, it would have been easier last week.

GOLDBERG. It would, eh?

MEG. Yes.

GOLDBERG. Why? How many have you got here at the moment?

MEG. Just one at the moment.

GOLDBERG. Just one?

MEG. Yes. Just one. Until you came.

GOLDBERG. And your husband, of course?

MEG. Yes, but he sleeps with me.

GOLDBERG. What does he do, your husband?

MEG. He's a deck-chair attendant.

GOLDBERG. Oh, very nice.

MEG. Yes, he's out in all weathers.

    She begins to take her purchases from her bag.

GOLDBERG. Of course. And your guest? Is he a man?

MEG. A man?

GOLDBERG. Or a woman?

MEG. No. A man.

GOLDBERG. Been here long?

MEG. He's been here about a year now.

GOLDBERG. Oh yes. A resident. What's his name?

MEG. Stanley Webber.

GOLDBERG. Oh yes? Does he work here?

MEG. He used to work. He used to be a pianist. In a concert party on the pier.

GOLDBERG. Oh yes? On the pier, eh? Does he play a nice piano?

MEG. Oh, lovely. (*She sits at the table.*) He once gave a concert.

GOLDBERG. Oh? Where?

MEG (*falteringly*). In . . . a big hall. His father gave him champagne. But then they locked the place up and he couldn't get out. The caretaker had gone home. So he had to wait until the morning before he could get out. (*With confidence.*) They were very grateful. (*Pause.*) And then they all wanted to give him a tip. And so he took the tip. And then he got a fast train and he came down here.

GOLDBERG. Really?

MEG. Oh yes. Straight down.

Pause.

MEG. I wish he could have played tonight.

GOLDBERG. Why tonight?

MEG. It's his birthday today.

GOLDBERG. His birthday?

MEG. Yes. Today. But I'm not going to tell him until tonight.

GOLDBERG. Doesn't he know it's his birthday?

MEG. He hasn't mentioned it.

GOLDBERG (*thoughtfully*). Ah! Tell me. Are you going to have a party?

MEG. A party?

GOLDBERG. Weren't you going to have one?

MEG (*her eyes wide*). No.

GOLDBERG. Well, of course, you must have one. (*He stands.*) We'll have a party, eh? What do you say?

MEG. Oh yes!

GOLDBERG. Sure. We'll give him a party. Leave it to me.

MEG. Oh, that's wonderful, Mr Gold—

GOLDBERG. Berg.

MEG. Berg.

GOLDBERG. You like the idea?

MEG. Oh, I'm so glad you came today.

GOLDBERG. If we hadn't come today we'd have come to-morrow. Still, I'm glad we came today. Just in time for his birthday.

MEG. I wanted to have a party But you must have people for a party.

GOLDBERG. And now you've got McCann and me. McCann's the life and soul of any party.

MCCANN. What?

GOLDBERG. What do you think of that, McCann? There's a gentleman living here. He's got a birthday today, and he's forgotten all about it. So we're going to remind him. We're going to give him a party.

MCCANN. Oh, is that a fact?

MEG. Tonight.

GOLDBERG. Tonight.

MEG. I'll put on my party dress.

GOLDBERG. And I'll get some bottles.

MEG. And I'll invite Lulu this afternoon. Oh, this is going to cheer Stanley up. It will. He's been down in the dumps lately.

GOLDBERG. We'll bring him out of himself.

MEG. I hope I look nice in my dress.

GOLDBERG. Madam, you'll look like a tulip.

MEG. What colour?

GOLDBERG. Er—well, I'll have to see the dress first.

MCCANN. Could I go up to my room?

MEG. Oh, I've put you both together. Do you mind being both together?

GOLDBERG. I don't mind. Do you mind, McCann?

MCCANN. No.

MEG. What time shall we have the party?

GOLDBERG. Nine o'clock.

MCCANN (*at the door*). Is this the way?

MEG (*rising*). I'll show you. If you don't mind coming upstairs.

GOLDBERG. With a tulip? It's a pleasure.

MEG *and* GOLDBERG *exit laughing, followed by* MCCANN. STANLEY *appears at the window. He enters by the back*

door. He goes to the door on the left, opens it and listens.
Silence, He walks to the table. He stands. He sits, as MEG
enters. She crosses and hangs her shopping bag on a hook. He
lights a match and watches it burn.

STANLEY. Who is it?

MEG. The two gentlemen.

STANLEY. What two gentlemen?

MEG. The ones that were coming. I just took them to their
room. They were thrilled with their room.

STANLEY. They've come?

MEG. They're very nice, Stan.

STANLEY. Why didn't they come last night?

MEG. They said the beds were wonderful.

STANLEY. Who are they?

MEG (*sitting*). They're very nice, Stanley.

STANLEY. I said, who are they?

MEG. I've told you, the two gentlemen.

STANLEY. I didn't think they'd come.

He rises and walks to the window.

MEG. They have. They were here when I came in.

STANLEY. What do they want here?

MEG. They want to stay.

STANLEY. How long for?

MEG. They didn't say.

STANLEY (*turning*). But why here? Why not somewhere else?

MEG. This house is on the list.

STANLEY (*coming down*). What are they called? What are their
names?

MEG. Oh, Stanley, I can't remember.

STANLEY. They told you, didn't they? Or didn't they tell you?

MEG. Yes, they. . . .

STANLEY. Then what are they? Come on. Try to remember.

MEG. Why, Stan? Do you know them?

STANLEY. How do I know if I know them until I know their
  names?
MEG. Well . . . he told me, I remember.
STANLEY. Well?

  She thinks.

MEG. Gold—something.
STANLEY. Goldsomething?
MEG. Yes. Gold. . . .
STANLEY. Yes?
MEG. Goldberg.
STANLEY. Goldberg?
MEG. That's right. That was one of them.

  STANLEY *slowly sits at the table, left.*

Do you know them?

  STANLEY *does not answer.*

Stan, they won't wake you up, I promise. I'll tell them they
must be quiet.

  STANLEY *sits still.*

They won't be here long, Stan. I'll still bring you up your
early morning tea.

  STANLEY *sits still.*

You mustn't be sad today. It's your birthday.

  A pause.

STANLEY (*dumbly*). Uh?
MEG. It's your birthday, Stan. I was going to keep it a secret
  until tonight.
STANLEY. No.
MEG. It is. I've brought you a present. (*She goes to the side-
  board, picks up the parcel, and places it on the table in front of
  him.*) Here. Go on. Open it.
STANLEY. What's this?

MEG. It's your present.

STANLEY. This isn't my birthday, Meg.

MEG. Of course it is. Open your present.

> *He stares at the parcel, slowly stands, and opens it. He takes out a boy's drum.*

STANLEY (*flatly*). It's a drum. A boy's drum.

MEG (*tenderly*). It's because you haven't got a piano. (*He stares at her, then turns and walks towards the door, left.*) Aren't you going to give me a kiss? (*He turns sharply, and stops. He walks back towards her slowly. He stops at her chair, looking down upon her. Pause. His shoulders sag, he bends and kisses her on the cheek.*) There are some sticks in there. (STANLEY *looks into the parcel. He takes out two drumsticks. He taps them together. He looks at her.*)

STANLEY. Shall I put it round my neck?

> *She watches him, uncertainly. He hangs the drum around his neck, taps it gently with the sticks, then marches round the table, beating it regularly.* MEG, *pleased, watches him. Still beating it regularly, he begins to go round the table a second time. Halfway round the beat becomes erratic, uncontrolled.* MEG *expresses dismay. He arrives at her chair, banging the drum, his face and the drumbeat now savage and possessed.*

> *Curtain*

Act Two

MCCANN *is sitting at the table tearing a sheet of newspaper into five equal strips. It is evening. After a few moments* STANLEY *enters from the left. He stops upon seeing* MCCANN, *and watches him. He then walks towards the kitchen, stops, and speaks.*

STANLEY. Evening.
MCCANN. Evening.

Chuckles are heard from outside the back door, which is open.

STANLEY. Very warm tonight. (*He turns towards the back door, and back.*) Someone out there?

MCCANN *tears another length of paper.* STANLEY *goes into the kitchen and pours a glass of water. He drinks it looking through the hatch. He puts the glass down, comes out of the kitchen and walks quickly towards the door, left.* MCCANN *rises and intercepts him.*

MCCANN. I don't think we've met.
STANLEY. No, we haven't.
MCCANN. My name's McCann.
STANLEY. Staying here long?
MCCANN. Not long. What's your name?
STANLEY. Webber.
MCCANN. I'm glad to meet you, sir. (*He offers his hand.* STANLEY *takes it, and* MCCANN *holds the grip.*) Many happy returns of the day. (STANLEY *withdraws his hand. They face each other.*) Were you going out?
STANLEY. Yes.
MCCANN. On your birthday?
STANLEY. Yes. Why not?

MCCANN. But they're holding a party here for you tonight.

STANLEY. Oh really? That's unfortunate.

MCCANN. Ah no. It's very nice.

Voices from outside the back door.

STANLEY. I'm sorry. I'm not in the mood for a party tonight.

MCCANN. Oh, is that so? I'm sorry.

STANLEY. Yes, I'm going out to celebrate quietly, on my own.

MCCANN. That's a shame.

They stand.

STANLEY. Well, if you'd move out of my way—

MCCANN. But everything's laid on. The guests are expected.

STANLEY. Guests? What guests?

MCCANN. Myself for one. I had the honour of an invitation.

MCCANN *begins to whistle "The Mountains of Morne".*

STANLEY (*moving away*). I wouldn't call it an honour, would you? It'll just be another booze-up.

STANLEY *joins* MCCANN *in whistling "The Mountains of Morne". During the next five lines the whistling is continuous, one whistling while the other speaks, and both whistling together.*

MCCANN. But it is an honour.

STANLEY. I'd say you were exaggerating.

MCCANN. Oh no. I'd say it was an honour.

STANLEY. I'd say that was plain stupid.

MCCANN. Ah no.

They stare at each other.

STANLEY. Who are the other guests?

MCCANN. A young lady.

STANLEY. Oh yes? And. . . .?

MCCANN. My friend.

STANLEY. Your friend?

MCCANN. That's right. It's all laid on.

> STANLEY *walks round the table towards the door.* MCCANN *meets him.*

STANLEY. Excuse me.

MCCANN. Where are you going?

STANLEY. I want to go out.

MCCANN. Why don't you stay here?

> STANLEY *moves away, to the right of the table.*

STANLEY. So you're down here on holiday?

MCCANN. A short one. (STANLEY *picks up a strip of paper.* MCCANN *moves in.*) Mind that.

STANLEY. What is it?

MCCANN. Mind it. Leave it.

STANLEY. I've got a feeling we've met before.

MCCANN. No we haven't.

STANLEY. Ever been anywhere near Maidenhead?

MCCANN. No.

STANLEY. There's a Fuller's teashop. I used to have my tea there.

MCCANN. I don't know it.

STANLEY. And a Boots Library. I seem to connect you with the High Street.

MCCANN. Yes?

STANLEY. A charming town, don't you think?

MCCANN. I don't know it.

STANLEY. Oh no. A quiet, thriving community. I was born and brought up there. I lived well away from the main road.

MCCANN. Yes?

> *Pause.*

STANLEY. You're here on a short stay?

MCCANN. That's right.

STANLEY. You'll find it very bracing.

MCCANN. Do you find it bracing?

STANLEY. Me? No. But you will. (*He sits at the table.*) I like
it here, but I'll be moving soon. Back home. I'll stay there
too, this time. No place like home. (*He laughs.*) I wouldn't
have left, but business calls. Business called, and I had to
leave for a bit. You know how it is.

MCCANN (*sitting at the table, left*). You in business?

STANLEY. No. I think I'll give it up. I've got a small private
income, you see. I think I'll give it up. Don't like being
away from home. I used to live very quietly—played records,
that's about all. Everything delivered to the door. Then I
started a little private business, in a small way, and it compelled me to come down here—kept me longer than I
expected. You never get used to living in someone else's
house. Don't you agree? I lived so quietly. You can only
appreciate what you've had when things change. That's what
they say, isn't it? Cigarette?

MCCANN. I don't smoke.

> STANLEY *lights a cigarette. Voices from the back.*

STANLEY. Who's out there?

MCCANN. My friend and the man of the house.

STANLEY. You know what? To look at me, I bet you wouldn't
think I'd led such a quiet life. The lines on my face, eh? It's
the drink. Been drinking a bit down here. But what I mean
is . . . you know how it is . . . away from your own . . .
all wrong, of course . . . I'll be all right when I get back
. . . but what I mean is, the way some people look at me
you'd think I was a different person. I suppose I have
changed, but I'm still the same man that I always was. I
mean, you wouldn't think, to look at me, really . . . I mean,
not really, that I was the sort of bloke to—to cause any
trouble, would you? (MCCANN *looks at him.*) Do you know
what I mean?

MCCANN. No. (*As* STANLEY *picks up a strip of paper.*) Mind
that.

STANLEY (*quickly*). Why are you down here?

MCCANN. A short holiday.

STANLEY. This is a ridiculous house to pick on. (*He rises.*)

MCCANN. Why?

STANLEY. Because it's not a boarding house. It never was.

MCCANN. Sure it is.

STANLEY. Why did you choose this house?

MCCANN. You know, sir, you're a bit depressed for a man on his birthday.

STANLEY (*sharply*). Why do you call me sir?

MCCANN. You don't like it?

STANLEY (*to the table.*) Listen. Don't call me sir.

MCCANN. I won't, if you don't like it.

STANLEY (*moving away*). No. Anyway, this isn't my birthday.

MCCANN. No?

STANLEY. No. It's not till next month.

MCCANN. Not according to the lady.

STANLEY. Her? She's crazy. Round the bend.

MCCANN. That's a terrible thing to say.

STANLEY (*to the table*). Haven't you found that out yet? There's a lot you don't know. I think someone's leading you up the garden path.

MCCANN. Who would do that?

STANLEY (*leaning across the table*). That woman is mad!

MCCANN. That's slander.

STANLEY. And you don't know what you're doing.

MCCANN. Your cigarette is near that paper.

Voices from the back.

STANLEY. Where the hell are they? (*Stubbing his cigarette.*) Why don't they come in? What are they doing out there?

MCCANN. You want to steady yourself.

STANLEY *crosses to him and grips his arm.*

STANLEY (*urgently*). Look—

MCCANN. Don't touch me.

STANLEY. Look. Listen a minute.

MCCANN. Let go my arm.

STANLEY. Look. Sit down a minute.

MCCANN (*savagely, hitting his arm*). Don't do that!

STANLEY *backs across the stage, holding his arm.*

STANLEY. Listen. You knew what I was talking about before, didn't you?

MCCANN. I don't know what you're at at all.

STANLEY. It's a mistake! Do you understand?

MCCANN. You're in a bad state, man.

STANLEY (*whispering, advancing*). Has he told you anything? Do you know what you're here for? Tell me. You needn't be frightened of me. Or hasn't he told you?

MCCANN. Told me what?

STANLEY (*hissing*). I've explained to you, damn you, that all those years I lived in Basingstoke I never stepped outside the door.

MCCANN. You know, I'm flabbergasted with you.

STANLEY (*reasonably*). Look. You look an honest man. You're being made a fool of, that's all. You understand? Where do you come from?

MCCANN. Where do you think?

STANLEY. I know Ireland very well. I've many friends there. I love that country and I admire and trust its people. I trust them. They respect the truth and they have a sense of humour. I think their policemen are wonderful. I've been there. I've never seen such sunsets. What about coming out to have a drink with me? There's a pub down the road serves draught Guinness. Very difficult to get in these parts —(*He breaks off. The voices draw nearer.* GOLDBERG *and* PETEY *enter from the back door.*)

GOLDBERG (*as he enters*). A mother in a million. (*He sees* STANLEY.) Ah.

PETEY. Oh hullo, Stan. You haven't met Stanley, have you, Mr Goldberg?

GOLDBERG. I haven't had the pleasure.

PETEY. Oh well, this is Mr Goldberg, this is Mr Webber.

GOLDBERG. Pleased to meet you.

PETEY. We were just getting a bit of air in the garden.

GOLDBERG. I was telling Mr Boles about my old mum. What days. (*He sits at the table, right.*) Yes. When I was a youngster, of a Friday, I used to go for a walk down the canal with a girl who lived down my road. A beautiful girl. What a voice that bird had! A nightingale, my word of honour. Good? Pure? She wasn't a Sunday school teacher for nothing. Anyway, I'd leave her with a little kiss on the cheek —I never took liberties—we weren't like the young men these days in those days. We knew the meaning of respect. So I'd give her a peck and I'd bowl back home. Humming away I'd be, past the children's playground. I'd tip my hat to the toddlers, I'd give a helping hand to a couple of stray dogs, everything came natural. I can see it like yesterday. The sun falling behind the dog stadium. Ah! (*He leans back contentedly.*)

MCCANN. Like behind the town hall.

GOLDBERG. What town hall?

MCCANN. In Carrikmacross.

GOLDBERG. There's no comparison. Up the street, into my gate, inside the door, home. "Simey!" my old mum used to shout, "quick before it gets cold." And there on the table what would I see? The nicest piece of gefilte fish you could wish to find on a plate.

MCCANN. I thought your name was Nat.

GOLDBERG. She called me Simey.

PETEY. Yes, we all remember our childhood.

GOLDBERG. Too true. Eh, Mr Webber, what do you say? Childhood. Hot water bottles. Hot milk. Pancakes. Soap suds. What a life.

Pause.

PETEY (*rising from the table*). Well, I'll have to be off.

GOLDBERG. Off?

PETEY. It's my chess night.

GOLDBERG. You're not staying for the party?

PETEY. No, I'm sorry, Stan. I didn't know about it till just
now. And we've got a game on. I'll try and get back early.

GOLDBERG. We'll save some drink for you, all right? Oh, that
reminds me. You'd better go and collect the bottles.

MCCANN. Now?

GOLDBERG. Of course, now. Time's getting on. Round the
corner, remember? Mention my name.

PETEY. I'm coming your way.

GOLDBERG. Beat him quick and come back, Mr Boles.

PETEY. Do my best. See you later, Stan.

> PETEY *and* MCCANN *go out, left.* STANLEY *moves to the
> centre.*

GOLDBERG. A warm night.

STANLEY (*turning*). Don't mess me about!

GOLDBERG. I beg your pardon?

STANLEY (*moving downstage*). I'm afraid there's been a mistake. We're booked out. Your room is taken. Mrs Boles
forgot to tell you. You'll have to find somewhere else.

GOLDBERG. Are you the manager here?

STANLEY. That's right.

GOLDBERG. Is it a good game?

STANLEY. I run the house. I'm afraid you and your friend will
have to find other accommodation.

GOLDBERG (*rising*). Oh, I forgot, I must congratulate you on
your birthday. (*Offering his hand.*) Congratulations.

STANLEY (*ignoring hand*). Perhaps you're deaf.

GOLDBERG. No, what makes you think that? As a matter of
fact, every single one of my senses is at its peak. Not bad
going, eh? For a man past fifty. But a birthday, I always feel,

is a great occasion, taken too much for granted these days. What a thing to celebrate—birth! Like getting up in the morning. Marvellous! Some people don't like the idea of getting up in the morning. I've heard them. Getting up in the morning, they say, what is it? Your skin's crabby, you need a shave, your eyes are full of muck, your mouth is like a boghouse, the palms of your hands are full of sweat, your nose is clogged up, your feet stink, what are you but a corpse waiting to be washed? Whenever I hear that point of view I feel cheerful. Because I know what it is to wake up with the sun shining, to the sound of the lawnmower, all the little birds, the smell of the grass, church bells, tomato juice—

STANLEY. Get out.

Enter MCCANN, *with bottles.*

Get that drink out. These are unlicensed premises.

GOLDBERG. You're in a terrible humour today, Mr Webber. And on your birthday too, with the good lady getting her strength up to give you a party.

MCCANN puts the bottles on the sideboard.

STANLEY. I told you to get those bottles out.

GOLDBERG. Mr Webber, sit down a minute.

STANLEY. Let me—just make this clear. You don't bother me. To me, you're nothing but a dirty joke. But I have a responsibility towards the people in this house. They've been down here too long. They've lost their sense of smell. I haven't. And nobody's going to take advantage of them while I'm here. (*A little less forceful.*) Anyway, this house isn't your cup of tea. There's nothing here for you, from any angle, any angle. So why don't you just go, without any more fuss?

GOLDBERG. Mr Webber, sit down.

STANLEY. It's no good starting any kind of trouble.

GOLDBERG. Sit down.

STANLEY. Why should I?

GOLDBERG. If you want to know the truth, Webber, you're beginning to get on my breasts.

STANLEY. Really? Well, that's—

GOLDBERG. Sit down.

STANLEY. No.

GOLDBERG *sighs, and sits at the table right.*

GOLDBERG. McCann.

MCCANN. Nat?

GOLDBERG. Ask him to sit down.

MCCANN. Yes, Nat. (MCCANN *moves to* STANLEY.) Do you mind sitting down?

STANLEY. Yes, I do mind.

MCCANN. Yes now, but—it'd be better if you did.

STANLEY. Why don't you sit down?

MCCANN. No, not me—you.

STANLEY. No thanks.

Pause.

MCCANN. Nat.

GOLDBERG. What?

MCCANN. He won't sit down.

GOLDBERG. Well, ask him.

MCCANN. I've asked him.

GOLDBERG. Ask him again.

MCCANN (*to* STANLEY). Sit down.

STANLEY. Why?

MCCANN. You'd be more comfortable.

STANLEY. So would you.

Pause.

MCCANN. All right. If you will I will.

STANLEY. You first.

MCCANN *slowly sits at the table, left*

MCCANN. Well?

STANLEY. Right. Now you've both had a rest you can get out!

MCCANN (*rising*). That's a dirty trick! I'll kick the shite out of him!

GOLDBERG (*rising*). No! I have stood up.

MCCANN. Sit down again!

GOLDBERG. Once I'm up I'm up.

STANLEY. Same here.

MCCANN (*moving to* STANLEY). You've made Mr Goldberg stand up.

STANLEY (*his voice rising*). It'll do him good!

MCCANN. Get in that seat.

GOLDBERG. McCann.

MCCANN. Get down in that seat!

GOLDBERG (*crossing to him*). Webber. (*Quietly.*) SIT DOWN. (*Silence.* STANLEY *begins to whistle "The Mountains of Morne". He strolls casually to the chair at the table. They watch him. He stops whistling. Silence. He sits.*)

STANLEY. You'd better be careful.

GOLDBERG. Webber, what were you doing yesterday?

STANLEY. Yesterday?

GOLDBERG. And the day before. What did you do the day before that?

STANLEY. What do you mean?

GOLDBERG. Why are you wasting everybody's time, Webber? Why are you getting in everybody's way?

STANLEY. Me? What are you—

GOLDBERG. I'm telling you, Webber. You're a washout. Why are you getting on everybody's wick? Why are you driving that old lady off her conk?

MCCANN. He likes to do it!

GOLDBERG. Why do you behave so badly, Webber? Why do you force that old man out to play chess?

STANLEY. Me?

GOLDBERG. Why do you treat that young lady like a leper?

She's not the leper, Webber!

STANLEY. What the—

GOLDBERG. What did you wear last week, Webber? Where do you keep your suits?

MCCANN. Why did you leave the organization?

GOLDBERG. What would your old mum say, Webber?

MCCANN. Why did you betray us?

GOLDBERG. You hurt me, Webber. You're playing a dirty game.

MCCANN. That's a Black and Tan fact.

GOLDBERG. Who does he think he is?

MCCANN. Who do you think you are?

STANLEY. You're on the wrong horse.

GOLDBERG. When did you come to this place?

STANLEY. Last year.

GOLDBERG. Where did you come from?

STANLEY. Somewhere else.

GOLDBERG. Why did you come here?

STANLEY. My feet hurt!

GOLDBERG. Why did you stay?

STANLEY. I had a headache!

GOLDBERG. Did you take anything for it?

STANLEY. Yes.

GOLDBERG. What?

STANLEY. Fruit salts!

GOLDBERG. Enos or Andrews?

STANLEY. En— An—

GOLDBERG. Did you stir properly? Did they fizz?

STANLEY. Now, now, wait, you—

GOLDBERG. Did they fizz? Did they fizz or didn't they fizz?

MCCANN. He doesn't know!

GOLDBERG. You don't know. When did you last have a bath?

STANLEY. I have one every—

GOLDBERG. Don't lie.

MCCANN. You betrayed the organization. I know him!

STANLEY. You don't!

GOLDBERG. What can you see without your glasses?

STANLEY. Anything.

GOLDBERG. Take off his glasses.

> MCCANN *snatches his glasses and as* STANLEY *rises, reaching for them, takes his chair downstage centre, below the table,* STANLEY *stumbling as he follows.* STANLEY *clutches the chair and stays bent over it.*

Webber, you're a fake. (*They stand on each side of the chair.*) When did you last wash up a cup?

STANLEY. The Christmas before last.

GOLDBERG. Where?

STANLEY. Lyons Corner House.

GOLDBERG. Which one?

STANLEY. Marble Arch.

GOLDBERG. Where was your wife?

STANLEY. In—

GOLDBERG. Answer.

STANLEY (*turning, crouched*). What wife?

GOLDBERG. What have you done with your wife?

MCCANN. He's killed his wife!

GOLDBERG. Why did you kill your wife?

STANLEY (*sitting, his back to the audience*). What wife?

MCCANN. How did he kill her?

GOLDBERG. How did you kill her?

MCCANN. You throttled her.

GOLDBERG. With arsenic.

MCCANN. There's your man!

GOLDBERG. Where's your old mum?

STANLEY. In the sanatorium.

MCCANN. Yes!

GOLDBERG. Why did you never get married?

MCCANN. She was waiting at the porch.

GOLDBERG. You skeddadled from the wedding.

MCCANN. He left her in the lurch.

GOLDBERG. You left her in the pudding club.

MCCANN. She was waiting at the church.

GOLDBERG. Webber! Why did you change your name?

STANLEY. I forgot the other one.

GOLDBERG. What's your name now?

STANLEY. Joe Soap.

GOLDBERG. You stink of sin.

MCCANN. I can smell it.

GOLDBERG. Do you recognise an external force?

STANLEY. What?

GOLDBERG. Do you recognise an external force?

MCCANN. That's the question!

GOLDBERG. Do you recognise an external force, responsible for you, suffering for you?

STANLEY. It's late.

GOLDBERG. Late! Late enough! When did you last pray?

MCCANN. He's sweating!

GOLDBERG. When did you last pray?

MCCANN. He's sweating!

GOLDBERG. Is the number 846 possible or necessary?

STANLEY. Neither.

GOLDBERG. Wrong! Is the number 846 possible or necessary?

STANLEY. Both.

GOLDBERG. Wrong! It's necessary but not possible.

STANLEY. Both.

GOLDBERG. Wrong! Why do you think the number 846 is necessarily possible?

STANLEY. Must be.

GOLDBERG. Wrong! It's only necessarily necessary! We admit possibility only after we grant necessity. It is possible because necessary but by no means necessary through possibility. The possibility can only be assumed after the proof of necessity.

MCCANN. Right!

GOLDBERG. Right? Of course right! We're right and you're wrong, Webber, all along the line.

MCCANN. All along the line!

GOLDBERG. Where is your lechery leading you?

MCCANN. You'll pay for this.

GOLDBERG. You stuff yourself with dry toast.

MCCANN. You contaminate womankind.

GOLDBERG. Why don't you pay the rent?

MCCANN. Mother defiler!

GOLDBERG. Why do you pick your nose?

MCCANN. I demand justice!

GOLDBERG. What's your trade?

MCCANN. What about Ireland?

GOLDBERG. What's your trade?

STANLEY. I play the piano.

GOLDBERG. How many fingers do you use?

STANLEY. No hands!

GOLDBERG. No society would touch you. Not even a building society.

MCCANN. You're a traitor to the cloth.

GOLDBERG. What do you use for pyjamas?

STANLEY. Nothing.

GOLDBERG. You verminate the sheet of your birth.

MCCANN. What about the Albigensenist heresy?

GOLDBERG. Who watered the wicket in Melbourne?

MCCANN. What about the blessed Oliver Plunkett?

GOLDBERG. Speak up, Webber. Why did the chicken cross the road?

STANLEY. He wanted to—he wanted to—he wanted to. . . .

MCCANN. He doesn't know!

GOLDBERG. Why did the chicken cross the road?

STANLEY. He wanted to—he wanted to. . . .

GOLDBERG. Why did the chicken cross the road?

STANLEY. He wanted. . . .

MCCANN. He doesn't know. He doesn't know which came first!

GOLDBERG. Which came first?

MCCANN. Chicken? Egg? Which came first?

GOLDBERG and MCCANN. Which came first? Which came first? Which came first?

> STANLEY *screams.*

GOLDBERG. He doesn't know. Do you know your own face?

MCCANN. Wake him up. Stick a needle in his eye.

GOLDBERG. You're a plague, Webber. You're an overthrow.

MCCANN. You're what's left!

GOLDBERG. But we've got the answer to you. We can sterilise you.

MCCANN. What about Drogheda?

GOLDBERG. Your bite is dead. Only your pong is left.

MCCANN. You betrayed our land.

GOLDBERG. You betray our breed.

MCCANN. Who are you, Webber?

GOLDBERG. What makes you think you exist?

MCCANN. You're dead.

GOLDBERG. You're dead. You can't live, you can't think, you can't love. You're dead. You're a plague gone bad. There's no juice in you. You're nothing but an odour!

> *Silence. They stand over him. He is crouched in the chair. He looks up slowly and kicks* GOLDBERG *in the stomach.* GOLDBERG *falls.* STANLEY *stands.* MCCANN *seizes a chair and lifts it above his head.* STANLEY *seizes a chair and covers his head with it.* MCCANN *and* STANLEY *circle.*

GOLDBERG. Steady, McCann.

STANLEY (*circling*). Uuuuuhhhhh!

MCCANN. Right, Judas.

GOLDBERG (*rising*). Steady, McCann.

MCCANN. Come on!

STANLEY. Uuuuuuuhhhhh!

MCCANN. He's sweating.

STANLEY. Uuuuuhhhhh!

GOLDBERG. Easy, McCann.

MCCANN. The bastard sweatpig is sweating.

A loud drumbeat off left, descending the stairs. GOLDBERG *takes the chair from* STANLEY. *They put the chairs down. They stop still. Enter* MEG, *in evening dress, holding sticks and drum.*

MEG. I brought the drum down. I'm dressed for the party.

GOLDBERG. Wonderful.

MEG. You like my dress?

GOLDBERG. Wonderful. Out of this world.

MEG. I know. My father gave it to me. (*Placing drum on table.*) Doesn't it make a beautiful noise?

GOLDBERG. It's a fine piece of work. Maybe Stan'll play us a little tune afterwards.

MEG. Oh yes. Will you, Stan?

STANLEY. Could I have my glasses?

GOLDBERG. Ah yes. (*He holds his hand out to* MCCANN. MCCANN *passes him his glasses.*) Here they are. (*He holds them out for* STANLEY, *who reaches for them.*) Here they are. (STANLEY *takes them.*) Now. What have we got here? Enough to scuttle a liner. We've got four bottles of Scotch and one bottle of Irish.

MEG. Oh, Mr Goldberg, what should I drink?

GOLDBERG. Glasses, glasses first. Open the Scotch, McCann.

MEG (*at the sideboard*). Here's my very best glasses in here.

MCCANN. I don't drink Scotch.

GOLDBERG. You've got the Irish.

MEG (*bringing the glasses*). Here they are.

GOLDBERG. Good. Mrs Boles, I think Stanley should pour the toast, don't you?

MEG. Oh yes. Come on, Stanley. (STANLEY *walks slowly to the table.*) Do you like my dress, Mr Goldberg?

GOLDBERG. It's out on its own. Turn yourself round a minute. I used to be in the business. Go on, walk up there.

MEG. Oh no.

GOLDBERG. Don't be shy. (*He slaps her bottom.*)

MEG. Ooooh!

GOLDBERG. Walk up the boulevard. Let's have a look at you. What a carriage. What's your opinion, McCann? Like a Countess, nothing less. Madam, now turn about and promenade to the kitchen. What a deportment!

MCCANN (*to* STANLEY). You can pour my Irish too.

GOLDBERG. You look like a Gladiola.

MEG. Stan, what about my dress?

GOLDBERG. One for the lady, one for the lady. Now madam— your glass.

MEG. Thank you.

GOLDBERG. Lift your glasses, ladies and gentlemen. We'll drink a toast.

MEG. Lulu isn't here.

GOLDBERG. It's past the hour. Now—who's going to propose the toast? Mrs Boles, it can only be you.

MEG. Me?

GOLDBERG. Who else?

MEG. But what do I say?

GOLDBERG. Say what you feel. What you honestly feel. (MEG *looks uncertain.*) It's Stanley's birthday. Your Stanley. Look at him. Look at him and it'll come. Wait a minute, the light's too strong. Let's have proper lighting. McCann, have you got your torch?

MCCANN (*bringing a small torch from his pocket*). Here.

GOLDBERG. Switch out the light and put on your torch. (MCCANN *goes to the door, switches off the light, comes back, shines the torch on* MEG. *Outside the window there is still a faint light.*) Not on the lady, on the gentleman! You must shine it on the birthday boy. (MCCANN *shines the torch in* STANLEY'S *face.*) Now, Mrs Boles, it's all yours.

　　Pause.

MEG. I don't know what to say.

GOLDBERG. Look at him. Just look at him.

MEG. Isn't the light in his eyes?

GOLDBERG. No, no. Go on.

MEG. Well—it's very, very nice to be here tonight, in my house, and I want to propose a toast to Stanley, because it's his birthday, and he's lived here for a long while now, and he's my Stanley now. And I think he's a good boy, although sometimes he's bad. (*An appreciative laugh from* GOLD-BERG.) And he's the only Stanley I know, and I know him better than all the world, although he doesn't think so. ("*Hear—hear" from* GOLDBERG.) Well, I could cry because I'm so happy, having him here and not gone away, on his birthday, and there isn't anything I wouldn't do for him, and all you good people here tonight. . . . (*She sobs.*)

GOLDBERG. Beautiful! A beautiful speech. Put the light on, McCann. (MCCANN *goes to the door.* STANLEY *remains still.*) That was a lovely toast. (*The light goes on.* LULU *enters from the door, left.* GOLDBERG *comforts* MEG.) Buck up now. Come on, smile at the birdy. That's better. Ah, look who's here.

MEG. Lulu.

GOLDBERG. How do you do, Lulu? I'm Nat Goldberg.

LULU. Hallo.

GOLDBERG. Stanley, a drink for your guest. You just missed the toast, my dear, and what a toast.

LULU. Did I?

GOLDBERG. Stanley, a drink for your guest. Stanley. (STAN-LEY *hands a glass to* LULU.) Right. Now raise your glasses. Everyone standing up? No, not you, Stanley. You must sit down.

MCCANN. Yes, that's right. He must sit down.

GOLDBERG. You don't mind sitting down a minute? We're going to drink to you.

MEG. Come on!

LULU. Come on!

STANLEY *sits in a chair at the table.*

GOLDBERG. Right. Now Stanley's sat down. (*Taking the stage.*) Well, I want to say first that I've never been so touched to the heart as by the toast we've just heard. How often, in this day and age, do you come across real, true warmth? Once in a lifetime. Until a few minutes ago, ladies and gentlemen, I, like all of you, was asking the same question. What's happened to the love, the bonhomie, the unashamed expression of affection of the day before yesterday, that our mums taught us in the nursery?

MCCANN. Gone with the wind.

GOLDBERG. That's what I thought, until today. I believe in a good laugh, a day's fishing, a bit of gardening. I was very proud of my old greenhouse, made out of my own spit and faith. That's the sort of man I am. Not size but quality. A little Austin, tea in Fullers, a library book from Boots, and I'm satisfied. But just now, I say just now, the lady of the house said her piece and I for one am knocked over by the sentiments she expressed. Lucky is the man who's at the receiving end, that's what I say. (*Pause.*) How can I put it to you? We all wander on our tod through this world. It's a lonely pillow to kip on. Right!

LULU (*admiringly*). Right!

GOLDBERG. Agreed. But tonight, Lulu, McCann, we've known a great fortune. We've heard a lady extend the sum total of her devotion, in all its pride, plume and peacock, to a member of her own living race. Stanley, my heartfelt congratulations. I wish you, on behalf of us all, a happy birthday. I'm sure you've never been a prouder man than you are today. Mazoltov! And may we only meet at Simchahs! (LULU *and* MEG *applaud.*) Turn out the light, McCann, while we drink the toast.

LULU. That was a wonderful speech.

MCCANN *switches out the light, comes back, and shines the torch in* STANLEY'S *face. The light outside the window is fainter.*

GOLDBERG. Lift your glasses. Stanley—happy birthday.

MCCANN. Happy birthday.

LULU. Happy birthday.

MEG. Many happy returns of the day, Stan.

GOLDBERG. And well over the fast.

They all drink.

MEG (*kissing him*). Oh, Stanny. . . .

GOLDBERG. Lights!

MCCANN. Right! (*He switches on the lights.*)

MEG. Clink my glass, Stan.

LULU. Mr Goldberg—

GOLDBERG. Call me Nat.

MEG (*to* MCCANN). You clink my glass.

LULU (*to* GOLDBERG). You're empty. Let me fill you up.

GOLDBERG. It's a pleasure.

LULU. You're a marvellous speaker, Nat, you know that? Where did you learn to speak like that?

GOLDBERG. You liked it, eh?

LULU. Oh yes!

GOLDBERG. Well, my first chance to stand up and give a lecture was at the Ethical Hall, Bayswater. A wonderful opportunity. I'll never forget it. They were all there that night. Charlotte Street was empty. Of course, that's a good while ago.

LULU. What did you speak about?

GOLDBERG. The Necessary and the Possible. It went like a bomb. Since then I always speak at weddings.

STANLEY *is still.* GOLDBERG *sits left of the table.* MEG *joins* MCCANN *downstage, right,* LULU *is downstage, left.* MCCANN *pours more Irish from the bottle, which he carries, into his glass.*

MEG. Let's have some of yours.

MCCANN. In that?

MEG. Yes.

MCCANN. Are you used to mixing them?

MEG. No.

MCCANN. Give me your glass.

> MEG *sits on a shoe-box, downstage, right.* LULU, *at the table, pours more drink for* GOLDBERG *and herself, and gives* GOLDBERG *his glass.*

GOLDBERG. Thank you.

MEG (*to* MCCANN). Do you think I should?

GOLDBERG. Lulu, you're a big bouncy girl. Come and sit on my lap.

MCCANN. Why not?

LULU. Do you think I should?

GOLDBERG. Try it.

MEG (*sipping*). Very nice.

LULU. I'll bounce up to the ceiling.

MCCANN. I don't know how you can mix that stuff.

GOLDBERG. Take a chance.

MEG (*to* MCCANN). Sit down on this stool.

> LULU *sits on* GOLDBERG'S *lap.*

MCCANN. This?

GOLDBERG. Comfortable?

LULU. Yes thanks.

MCCANN (*sitting*). It's comfortable.

GOLDBERG. You know, there's a lot in your eyes.

LULU. And in yours, too.

GOLDBERG. Do you think so?

LULU (*giggling*). Go on!

MCCANN (*to* MEG). Where'd you get it?

MEG. My father gave it to me.

LULU. I didn't know I was going to meet you here tonight.

MCCANN (*to* MEG). Ever been to Carrikmacross?

MEG (*drinking*). I've been to King's Cross.

LULU. You came right out of the blue, you know that?

GOLDBERG (*as she moves*). Mind how you go. You're cracking a rib.

MEG (*standing*). I want to dance! (LULU *and* GOLDBERG *look into each other's eyes.* MCCANN *drinks.* MEG *crosses to* STANLEY). Stanley. Dance. (STANLEY *sits still.* MEG *dances round the room alone, then comes back to* MCCANN, *who fills her glass. She sits.*)

LULU (*to* GOLDBERG). Shall I tell you something?

GOLDBERG. What?

LULU. I trust you.

GOLDBERG (*lifting his glass*). Gesundheit.

LULU. Have you got a wife?

GOLDBERG. I had a wife. What a wife. Listen to this. Friday, of an afternoon, I'd take myself for a little constitutional, down over the park. Eh, do me a favour, just sit on the table a minute, will you? (LULU *sits on the table. He stretches and continues.*) A little constitutional. I'd say hullo to the little boys, the little girls—I never made distinctions—and then back I'd go, back to my bungalow with the flat roof. "Simey," my wife used to shout, "quick, before it gets cold!" And there on the table what would I see? The nicest piece of roll-mop and pickled cucumber you could wish to find on a plate,

LULU. I thought your name was Nat.

GOLDBERG. She called me Simey.

LULU. I bet you were a good husband.

GOLDBERG. You should have seen her funeral.

LULU. Why?

GOLDBERG (*draws in his breath and wags head*). What a funeral.

MEG (*to* MCCANN). My father was going to take me to Ireland once. But then he went away by himself.

LULU (*to* GOLDBERG). Do you think you knew me when I was a little girl?

GOLDBERG. Were you a nice little girl?

LULU. I was.

MEG. I don't know if he went to Ireland.

GOLDBERG. Maybe I played piggy-back with you.

LULU. Maybe you did.

MEG. He didn't take me.

GOLDBERG. Or pop goes the weasel.

LULU. Is that a game?

GOLDBERG. Sure it's a game!

MCCANN. Why didn't he take you to Ireland?

LULU. You're tickling me!

GOLDBERG. You should worry.

LULU. I've always liked older men. They can soothe you.

They embrace.

MCCANN. I know a place. Roscrea. Mother Nolan's.

MEG. There was a night-light in my room, when I was a little girl.

MCCANN. One time I stayed there all night with the boys. Singing and drinking all night.

MEG. And my Nanny used to sit up with me, and sing songs to me.

MCCANN. And a plate of fry in the morning. Now where am I?

MEG. My little room was pink. I had a pink carpet and pink curtains, and I had musical boxes all over the room. And they played me to sleep. And my father was a very big doctor. That's why I never had any complaints. I was cared for, and I had little sisters and brothers in other rooms, all different colours.

MCCANN. Tullamore, where are you?

MEG (*to* MCCANN). Give us a drop more.

MCCANN (*filling her glass and singing*). Glorio, Glorio, to the bold Fenian men!

MEG. Oh, what a lovely voice.

GOLDBERG. Give us a song, McCann.

LULU. A love song!

MCCANN (*reciting*). The night that poor Paddy was stretched, the boys they all paid him a visit.

GOLDBERG. A love song!

MCCANN (*in a full voice, sings*)

> Oh, the Garden of Eden has vanished, they say,
> But I know the lie of it still.
> Just turn to the left at the foot of Ben Clay
> And stop when halfway to Coote Hill.
> It's there you will find it, I know sure enough,
> And it's whispering over to me:
> Come back, Paddy Reilly, to Bally-James-Duff,
> Come home, Paddy Reilly, to me!

LULU (*to* GOLDBERG). You're the dead image of the first man I ever loved.

GOLDBERG. It goes without saying.

MEG (*rising*). I want to play a game!

GOLDBERG. A game?

LULU. What game?

MEG. Any game.

LULU (*jumping up*). Yes, let's play a game.

GOLDBERG. What game?

MCCANN. Hide and seek.

LULU. Blind man's buff.

MEG. Yes!

GOLDBERG. You want to play blind man's buff?

LULU and MEG. Yes!

GOLDBERG. All right. Blind man's buff. Come on! Everyone up! (*Rising.*) McCann. Stanley—Stanley!

MEG. Stanley. Up.

GOLDBERG. What's the matter with him?

MEG (*bending over him*). Stanley, we're going to play a game. Oh, come on, don't be sulky, Stan.

LULU. Come on.

> STANLEY *rises.* MCCANN *rises.*

GOLDBERG. Right! Now—who's going to be blind first?

LULU. Mrs Boles.

MEG. Not me.

GOLDBERG. Of course you.

MEG. Who, me?

LULU (*taking her scarf from her neck*). Here you are.

MCCANN. How do you play this game?

LULU (*tying her scarf round* MEG'S *eyes*). Haven't you ever played blind man's buff? Keep still, Mrs Boles. You mustn't be touched. But you can't move after she's blind. You must stay where you are after she's blind. And if she touches you then you become blind. Turn round. How many fingers am I holding up?

MEG. I can't see.

LULU. Right.

GOLDBERG. Right! Everyone move about. McCann. Stanley. Now stop. Now still. Off you go!

> STANLEY *is downstage, right,* MEG *moves about the room.* GOLDBERG *fondles* LULU *at arm's length.* MEG *touches* MCCANN.

MEG. Caught you!

LULU. Take off your scarf.

MEG. What lovely hair!

LULU (*untying the scarf*). There.

MEG. It's you!

GOLDBERG. Put it on, McCann.

LULU (*tying it on* MCCANN). There. Turn round. How many fingers am I holding up?

MCCANN. I don't know.

GOLDBERG. Right! Everyone move about. Right. Stop! Still!

> MCCANN *begins to move.*

MEG. Oh, this is lovely!

GOLDBERG. Quiet! Tch, tch, tch. Now—all move again. Stop! Still!

> MCCANN *moves about.* GOLDBERG *fondles* LULU *at arm's length.* MCCANN *draws near* STANLEY. *He stretches his arm and touches* STANLEY'S *glasses.*

MEG. It's Stanley!

GOLDBERG (*to* LULU). Enjoying the game?

MEG. It's your turn, Stan.

> MCCANN *takes off the scarf.*

MCCANN (*to* STANLEY). I'll take your glasses.

> MCCANN *takes* STANLEY'S *glasses.*

MEG. Give me the scarf.

GOLDBERG (*holding* LULU). Tie his scarf, Mrs. Boles.

MEG. That's what I'm doing. (*To* STANLEY.) Can you see my nose?

GOLDBERG. He can't. Ready? Right! Everyone move. Stop! And still!

> STANLEY *stands blindfold.* MCCANN *backs slowly across the stage to the left. He breaks* STANLEY'S *glasses, snapping the frames.* MEG *is downstage, left,* LULU *and* GOLDBERG *upstage centre, close together.* STANLEY *begins to move, very slowly, across the stage to the left.* MCCANN *picks up the drum and places it sideways in* STANLEY'S *path.* STANLEY *walks into the drum and falls over with his foot caught in it.*

MEG. Ooh!

GOLDBERG. Sssh!

> STANLEY *rises. He begins to move towards* MEG, *dragging the drum on his foot. He reaches her and stops. His hands*

*move towards her and they reach her throat. He begins to
strangle her.* MCCANN *and* GOLDBERG *rush forward and
throw him off.*

BLACKOUT

*There is now no light at all through the window. The stage
is in darkness.*

LULU. The lights!

GOLDBERG. What's happened?

LULU. The lights!

MCCANN. Wait a minute.

GOLDBERG. Where is he?

MCCANN. Let go of me!

GOLDBERG. Who's this?

LULU. Someone's touching me!

MCCANN. Where is he?

MEG. Why has the light gone out?

GOLDBERG. Where's your torch? (MCCANN *shines the torch in*
GOLDBERG'S *face.*) Not on me! (MCCANN *shifts the torch.
It is knocked from his hand and falls. It goes out.*)

MCCANN. My torch!

LULU. Oh God!

GOLDBERG. Where's your torch? Pick up your torch!

MCCANN. I can't find it.

LULU. Hold me. Hold me.

GOLDBERG. Get down on your knees. Help him find the torch.

LULU. I can't.

MCCANN. It's gone.

MEG. Why has the light gone out?

GOLDBERG. Everyone quiet! Help him find the torch.

Silence. Grunts from MCCANN *and* GOLDBERG *on their
knees. Suddenly there is a sharp, sustained rat-a-tat with a
stick on the side of the drum from the back of the room.
Silence. Whimpers from* LULU.

GOLDBERG. Over here. McCann!

MCCANN. Here.

GOLDBERG. Come to me, come to me. Easy. Over there.

    GOLDBERG *and* MCCANN *move up left of the table.* STANLEY *moves down right of the table.* LULU *suddenly perceives him moving towards her, screams and faints.* GOLDBERG *and* MCCANN *turn and stumble against each other.*

GOLDBERG. What is it?

MCCANN. Who's that?

GOLDBERG. What is it?

    In the darkness STANLEY *picks up* LULU *and places her on the table.*

MEG. It's Lulu!

    GOLDBERG *and* MCCANN *move downstage, right.*

GOLDBERG. Where is she?

MCCANN. She fell.

GOLDBERG. Where?

MCCANN. About here.

GOLDBERG. Help me pick her up.

MCCANN (*moving downstage, left*). I can't find her.

GOLDBERG. She must be somewhere.

MCCANN. She's not here.

GOLDBERG (*moving downstage, left*). She must be.

MCCANN. She's gone.

    MCCANN *finds the torch on the floor, shines it on the table and* STANLEY. LULU *is lying spread-eagled on the table,* STANLEY *bent over her.* STANLEY, *as soon as the torchlight hits him, begins to giggle.* GOLDBERG *and* MCCANN *move towards him. He backs, giggling, the torch on his face. They follow him upstage, left. He backs against the hatch, giggling. The torch draws closer. His giggle rises and grows as he flattens himself against the wall. Their figures converge upon him.*

Curtain

Act Three

The next morning. PETEY *enters, left, with a newspaper and sits at the table. He begins to read.* MEG'S *voice comes through the kitchen hatch.*

MEG. Is that you, Stan? (*Pause.*) Stanny?

PETEY. Yes?

MEG. Is that you?

PETEY. It's me.

MEG (*appearing at the hatch*). Oh, it's you. I've run out of cornflakes.

PETEY. Well, what else have you got?

MEG. Nothing.

PETEY. Nothing?

MEG. Just a minute. (*She leaves the hatch and enters by the kitchen door.*) You got your paper?

PETEY. Yes.

MEG. Is it good?

PETEY. Not bad.

MEG. The two gentlemen had the last of the fry this morning.

PETEY. Oh, did they?

MEG. There's some tea in the pot though. (*She pours tea for him.*) I'm going out shopping in a minute. Get you something nice. I've got a splitting headache.

PETEY (*reading*). You slept like a log last night.

MEG. Did I?

PETEY. Dead out.

MEG. I must have been tired. (*She looks about the room and sees the broken drum in the fireplace.*) Oh, look. (*She rises and picks it up.*) The drum's broken. (PETEY *looks up.*) Why is it broken?

PETEY. I don't know.

She hits it with her hand.

MEG. It still makes a noise.

PETEY. You can always get another one.

MEG (*sadly*). It was probably broken in the party. I don't remember it being broken though, in the party. (*She puts it down.*) What a shame.

PETEY. You can always get another one, Meg.

MEG. Well, at least he did have it on his birthday, didn't he? Like I wanted him to.

PETEY (*reading*). Yes.

MEG. Have you seen him down yet? (PETEY *does not answer.*) Petey.

PETEY. What?

MEG. Have you seen him down?

PETEY. Who?

MEG. Stanley.

PETEY. No.

MEG. Nor have I. That boy should be up. He's late for his breakfast.

PETEY. There isn't any breakfast.

MEG. Yes, but he doesn't know that. I'm going to call him.

PETEY (*quickly*). No, don't do that, Meg. Let him sleep.

MEG. But you say he stays in bed too much.

PETEY. Let him sleep . . . this morning. Leave him.

MEG. I've been up once, with his cup of tea. But Mr McCann opened the door. He said they were talking. He said he'd made him one. He must have been up early. I don't know what they were talking about. I was surprised. Because Stanley's usually fast asleep when I wake him. But he wasn't this morning. I heard him talking. (*Pause.*) Do you think they know each other? I think they're old friends. Stanley had a lot of friends. I know he did. (*Pause.*) I didn't give him his tea. He'd already had one. I came down again

and went on with my work. Then, after a bit, they came
down to breakfast. Stanley must have gone to sleep again.

Pause.

PETEY. When are you going to do your shopping, Meg?

MEG. Yes, I must. (*Collecting the bag.*) I've got a rotten headache. (*She goes to the back door, stops suddenly and turns.*)
Did you see what's outside this morning?

PETEY. What?

MEG. That big car.

PETEY. Yes.

MEG. It wasn't there yesterday. Did you . . . did you have a
look inside it?

PETEY. I had a peep.

MEG (*coming down tensely, and whispering*). Is there anything
in it?

PETEY. In it?

MEG. Yes.

PETEY. What do you mean, in it?

MEG. Inside it.

PETEY. What sort of thing?

MEG. Well . . . I mean . . . is there . . . is there a wheelbarrow
in it?

PETEY. A wheelbarrow?

MEG. Yes.

PETEY. I didn't see one.

MEG. You didn't? Are you sure?

PETEY. What would Mr Goldberg want with a wheelbarrow?

MEG. Mr Goldberg?

PETEY. It's his car.

MEG (*relieved*). His car? Oh, I didn't know it was his car.

PETEY. Of course it's his car.

MEG. Oh, I feel better.

PETEY. What are you on about?

MEG. Oh, I do feel better.

PETEY. You go and get a bit of air.

MEG. Yes, I will. I will. I'll go and get the shopping. (*She goes towards the back door. A door slams upstairs. She turns.*) It's Stanley! He's coming down—what am I going to do about his breakfast? (*She rushes into the kitchen.*) Petey, what shall I give him? (*She looks through the hatch.*) There's no corn-flakes. (*They both gaze at the door. Enter* GOLDBERG. *He halts at the door, as he meets their gaze, then smiles.*)

GOLDBERG. A reception committee!

MEG. Oh, I thought it was Stanley.

GOLDBERG. You find a resemblance?

MEG. Oh no. You look quite different.

GOLDBERG (*coming into the room*). Different build, of course.

MEG (*entering from the kitchen*). I thought he was coming down for his breakfast. He hasn't had his breakfast yet.

GOLDBERG. Your wife makes a very nice cup of tea, Mr Boles, you know that?

PETEY. Yes, she does sometimes. Sometimes she forgets.

MEG. Is he coming down?

GOLDBERG. Down? Of course he's coming down. On a lovely sunny day like this he shouldn't come down? He'll be up and about in next to no time. (*He sits at the table.*) And what a breakfast he's going to get.

MEG. Mr Goldberg.

GOLDBERG. Yes?

MEG. I didn't know that was your car outside.

GOLDBERG. You like it?

MEG. Are you going to go for a ride?

GOLDBERG (*to* PETEY). A smart car, eh?

PETEY. Nice shine on it all right.

GOLDBERG. What is old is good, take my tip. There's room there. Room in the front, and room in the back. (*He strokes the teapot.*) The pot's hot. More tea, Mr Boles?

PETEY. No thanks.

GOLDBERG (*pouring tea*). That car? That car's never let me

down.

MEG. Are you going to go for a ride?

GOLDBERG *does not answer, drinks his tea.*

MEG. Well, I'd better be off now. (*She moves to the back door, and turns.*) Petey, when Stanley comes down. . . .

PETEY. Yes?

MEG. Tell him I won't be long.

PETEY. I'll tell him.

MEG (*vaguely*). I won't be long. (*She exits.*)

GOLDBERG (*sipping his tea*). A good woman. A charming woman. My mother was the same. My wife was identical.

PETEY. How is he this morning?

GOLDBERG. Who?

PETEY. Stanley. Is he any better?

GOLDBERG (*a little uncertainly*). Oh . . . a little better, I think, a little better. Of course, I'm not really qualified to say, Mr Boles. I mean, I haven't got the . . . the qualifications. The best thing would be if someone with the proper . . . mnn . . . qualifications . . . was to have a look at him. Someone with a few letters after his name. It makes all the difference.

PETEY. Yes.

GOLDBERG. Anyway, Dermot's with him at the moment. He's . . . keeping him company.

PETEY. Dermot?

GOLDBERG. Yes.

PETEY. It's a terrible thing.

GOLDBERG (*sighs*). Yes. The birthday celebration was too much for him.

PETEY. What came over him?

GOLDBERG (*sharply*). What came over him? Breakdown, Mr Boles. Pure and simple. Nervous breakdown.

PETEY. But what brought it on so suddenly?

GOLDBERG (*rising, and moving upstage*). Well, Mr Boles, it can happen in all sorts of ways. A friend of mine was telling me about it only the other day. We'd both been concerned with another case—not entirely similar, of course, but . . . quite alike, quite alike. (*He pauses.*) Anyway, he was telling me, you see, this friend of mine, that sometimes it happens gradual—day by day it grows and grows and grows . . . day by day. And then other times it happens all at once. Poof! Like that! The nerves break. There's no guarantee how it's going to happen, but with certain people . . . it's a foregone conclusion.

PETEY. Really?

GOLDBERG. Yes. This friend of mine—he was telling me about it—only the other day. (*He stands uneasily for a moment, then brings out a cigarette case and takes a cigarette.*) Have an Abdullah.

PETEY. No, no, I don't take them.

GOLDBERG. Once in a while I treat myself to a cigarette. An Abdullah, perhaps, or a . . . (*He snaps his fingers.*)

PETEY. What a night. (GOLDBERG *lights his cigarette with a lighter.*) Came in the front door and all the lights were out. Put a shilling in the slot, came in here and the party was over.

GOLDBERG (*coming downstage*). You put a shilling in the slot?

PETEY. Yes.

GOLDBERG. And the lights came on.

PETEY. Yes, then I came in here.

GOLDBERG (*with a short laugh*). I could have sworn it was a fuse.

PETEY (*continuing*). There was dead silence. Couldn't hear a thing. So I went upstairs and your friend—Dermot—met me on the landing. And he told me.

GOLDBERG (*sharply*). Who?

PETEY. Your friend—Dermot.

GOLDBERG (*heavily*). Dermot. Yes. (*He sits.*)

PETEY. They get over it sometimes though, don't they? I mean, they can recover from it, can't they?

GOLDBERG. Recover? Yes, sometimes they recover, in one way or another.

PETEY. I mean, he might have recovered by now, mightn't he?

GOLDBERG. It's conceivable. Conceivable.

PETEY rises and picks up the teapot and cup.

PETEY. Well, if he's no better by lunchtime I'll go and get hold of a doctor.

GOLDBERG (*briskly*). It's all taken care of, Mr Boles. Don't worry yourself.

PETEY (*dubiously*). What do you mean? (*Enter MCCANN with two suitcases.*) All packed up?

PETEY takes the teapot and cups into the kitchen. MCCANN crosses left and puts down the suitcases. He goes up to the window and looks out.

GOLDBERG. Well? (*MCCANN does not answer.*) McCann. I asked you well.

MCCANN (*without turning*). Well what?

GOLDBERG. What's what? (*MCCANN does not answer.*)

MCCANN (*turning to look at GOLDBERG, grimly*). I'm not going up there again.

GOLDBERG. Why not?

MCCANN. I'm not going up there again.

GOLDBERG. What's going on now?

MCCANN (*moving down*). He's quiet now. He stopped all that . . . talking a while ago.

PETEY appears at the kitchen hatch, unnoticed.

GOLDBERG. When will he be ready?

MCCANN (*sullenly*). You can go up yourself next time.

GOLDBERG. What's the matter with you?

MCCANN (*quietly*). I gave him. . . .

GOLDBERG. What?

MCCANN. I gave him his glasses.

GOLDBERG. Wasn't he glad to get them back?

MCCANN. The frames are bust.

GOLDBERG. How did that happen?

MCCANN. He tried to fit the eyeholes into his eyes. I left him doing it.

PETEY (*at the kitchen door*). There's some Sellotape somewhere. We can stick them together.

GOLDBERG *and* MCCANN *turn to see him. Pause.*

GOLDBERG. Sellotape? No, no, that's all right, Mr Boles. It'll keep him quiet for the time being, keep his mind off other things.

PETEY (*moving downstage*). What about a doctor?

GOLDBERG. It's all taken care of.

MCCANN *moves over right to the shoe-box, and takes out a brush and brushes his shoes.*

PETEY (*moves to the table*). I think he needs one.

GOLDBERG. I agree with you. It's all taken care of. We'll give him a bit of time to settle down, and then I'll take him to Monty.

PETEY. You're going to take him to a doctor?

GOLDBERG (*staring at him*). Sure. Monty.

Pause. MCCANN *brushes his shoes.*

So Mrs Boles has gone out to get us something nice for lunch?

PETEY. That's right.

GOLDBERG. Unfortunately we may be gone by then.

PETEY. Will you?

GOLDBERG. By then we may be gone.

Pause.

PETEY. Well, I think I'll see how my peas are getting on, in the meantime.

GOLDBERG. The meantime?

PETEY. While we're waiting.

GOLDBERG. Waiting for what? (PETEY *walks towards the back door*.) Aren't you going back to the beach?

PETEY. No, not yet. Give me a call when he comes down, will you, Mr Goldberg?

GOLDBERG (*earnestly*). You'll have a crowded beach today . . . on a day like this. They'll be lying on their backs, swimming out to sea. My life. What about the deck-chairs? Are the deck-chairs ready?

PETEY. I put them all out this morning.

GOLDBERG. But what about the tickets? Who's going to take the tickets?

PETEY. That's all right. That'll be all right. Mr Goldberg. Don't you worry about that. I'll be back.

He exits. GOLDBERG *rises, goes to the window and looks after him.* MCCANN *crosses to the table, left, sits, picks up the paper and begins to tear it into strips.*

GOLDBERG. Is everything ready?

MCCANN. Sure.

GOLDBERG *walks heavily, brooding, to the table. He sits right of it noticing what* MCCANN *is doing.*

GOLDBERG. Stop doing that!

MCCANN. What?

GOLDBERG. Why do you do that all the time? It's childish, it's pointless. It's without a solitary point.

MCCANN. What's the matter with you today?

GOLDBERG. Questions, questions. Stop asking me so many questions. What do you think I am?

MCCANN *studies him. He then folds the paper, leaving the strips inside.*

MCCANN. Well?

Pause. GOLDBERG *leans back in the chair, his eyes closed.*

MCCANN. Well?

GOLDBERG (*with fatigue*). Well what?

MCCANN. Do we wait or do we go and get him?

GOLDBERG (*slowly*). You want to go and get him?

MCCANN. I want to get it over.

GOLDBERG. That's understandable.

MCCANN. So do we wait or do we go and get him?

GOLDBERG (*interrupting*). I don't know why, but I feel knocked out. I feel a bit . . . It's uncommon for me.

MCCANN. Is that so?

GOLDBERG. It's unusual.

MCCANN (*rising swiftly and going behind* GOLDBERG'S *chair. Hissing*). Let's finish and go. Let's get it over and go. Get the thing done. Let's finish the bloody thing. Let's get the thing done and go!

Pause.

Will I go up?

Pause.

Nat!

GOLDBERG *sits humped.* MCCANN *slips to his side.*

Simey!

GOLDBERG (*opening his eyes, regarding* MCCANN). What—did —you—call—me?

MCCANN. Who?

GOLDBERG (*murderously*). Don't call me that! (*He seizes* MCCANN *by the throat.*) NEVER CALL ME THAT!

MCCANN (*writhing*). Nat, Nat, Nat, NAT! I called you Nat. I was asking you, Nat. Honest to God. Just a question, that's all, just a question, do you see, do you follow me?

GOLDBERG (*jerking him away*). What question?

MCCANN. Will I go up?

GOLDBERG (*violently*). Up? I thought you weren't going to go up there again?

MCCANN. What do you mean? Why not?

GOLDBERG. You said so!

MCCANN. I never said that!

GOLDBERG. No?

MCCANN (*from the floor, to the room at large*). Who said that? I never said that! I'll go up now!

He jumps up and rushes to the door, left.

GOLDBERG. Wait!

He stretches his arms to the arms of the chair.

Come here.

MCCANN approaches him very slowly.

I want your opinion. Have a look in my mouth.

He opens his mouth wide.

Take a good look.

MCCANN looks.

You know what I mean?

MCCANN peers.

You know what? I've never lost a tooth. Not since the day I was born. Nothing's changed. (*He gets up.*) That's why I've reached my position, McCann. Because I've always been as fit as a fiddle. All my life I've said the same. Play up, play up, and play the game. Honour thy father and thy mother. All along the line. Follow the line, the line, McCann, and you can't go wrong. What do you think, I'm a self-made man? No! I sat where I was told to sit. I kept my eye on the ball. School? Don't talk to me about school. Top in all subjects. And for why? Because I'm telling you, I'm telling you, follow my line? Follow my mental? Learn by heart. Never write down a thing. And don't go too near the water.

And you'll find—that what I say is true.
Because I believe that the world . . . (*Vacant.*). . . .
Because I believe that the world . . . (*Desperate.*). . . .
BECAUSE I BELIEVE THAT THE WORLD . . . (*Lost.*). . . .

He sits in chair.

Sit down, McCann, sit here where I can look at you.

MCCANN *kneels in front of the table.*

(*Intensely, with growing certainty.*) My father said to me,
Benny, Benny, he said, come here. He was dying. I knelt
down. By him day and night. Who else was there? Forgive,
Benny, he said, and let live. Yes, Dad. Go home to your wife.
I will, Dad. Keep an eye open for low-lives, for schnorrers
and for layabouts. He didn't mention names. I lost my life
in the service of others, he said, I'm not ashamed. Do your
duty and keep your observations. Always bid good morning
to the neighbours. Never, never forget your family, for they
are the rock, the constitution and the core! If you're ever in
any difficulties Uncle Barney will see you in the clear. I knelt
down. (*He kneels, facing* MCCANN.) I swore on the good
book. And I knew the word I had to remember—Respect!
Because McCann— (*Gently.*) Seamus—who came before
your father? His father. And who came before him? Before
him? . . . (*Vacant—triumphant.*) Who came before your
father's father but your father's father's mother! Your
great-gran-granny.

Silence. He slowly rises.

And that's why I've reached my position, McCann. Because
I've always been as fit as a fiddle. My motto. Work hard and
play hard. Not a day's illness.

GOLDBERG *sits.*

GOLDBERG. All the same, give me a blow. (*Pause.*) Blow in my mouth.

> MCCANN *stands, puts his hands on his knees, bends, and blows in* GOLDBERG'S *mouth.*

One for the road.

> MCCANN *blows again in his mouth.* GOLDBERG *breathes deeply, smiles.*

GOLDBERG. Right!

> *Enter* LULU. MCCANN *looks at them, and goes to the door.*

MCCANN (*at the door*). I'll give you five minutes. (*He exits.*)

GOLDBERG. Come over here.

LULU. What's going to happen?

GOLDBERG. Come over here.

LULU. No, thank you.

GOLDBERG. What's the matter? You got the needle to Uncle Natey?

LULU. I'm going.

GOLDBERG. Have a game of pontoon first, for old time's sake.

LULU. I've had enough games.

GOLDBERG. A girl like you, at your age, at your time of health, and you don't take to games?

LULU. You're very smart.

GOLDBERG. Anyway, who says you don't take to them?

LULU. Do you think I'm like all the other girls?

GOLDBERG. Are all the other girls like that, too?

LULU. I don't know about any other girls.

GOLDBERG. Nor me. I've never touched another woman.

LULU (*distressed*). What would my father say, if he knew? And what would Eddie say?

GOLDBERG. Eddie?

LULU. He was my first love, Eddie was. And whatever happened, it was pure. With him! He didn't come into my room at night with a briefcase!

GOLDBERG. Who opened the briefcase, me or you? Lulu, schmulu, let bygones be bygones, do me a turn. Kiss and make up.

LULU. I wouldn't touch you.

GOLDBERG. And today I'm leaving.

LULU. You're leaving?

GOLDBERG. Today.

LULU (*with growing anger*). You used me for a night. A passing fancy.

GOLDBERG. Who used who?

LULU. You made use of me by cunning when my defences were down.

GOLDBERG. Who took them down?

LULU. That's what you did. You quenched your ugly thirst. You taught me things a girl shouldn't know before she's been married at least three times!

GOLDBERG. Now you're a jump ahead! What are you complaining about?

Enter MCCANN *quickly.*

LULU. You didn't appreciate me for myself. You took all those liberties only to satisfy your appetite. Oh Nat, why did you do it?

GOLDBERG. You wanted me to do it, Lulula, so I did it.

MCCANN. That's fair enough. (*Advancing.*) You had a long sleep, Miss.

LULU (*backing upstage left*). Me?

MCCANN. Your sort, you spend too much time in bed.

LULU. What do you mean?

MCCANN. Have you got anything to confess?

LULU. What?

MCCANN (*savagely*). Confess!

LULU. Confess what?

MCCANN. Down on your knees and confess!

LULU. What does he mean?

GOLDBERG. Confess. What can you lose?

LULU. What, to him?

GOLDBERG. He's only been unfrocked six months.

MCCANN. Kneel down, woman, and tell me the latest!

LULU (*retreating to the back door*). I've seen everything that's happened. I know what's going on. I've got a pretty shrewd idea.

MCCANN (*advancing*). I've seen you hanging about the Rock of Cashel, profaning the soil with your goings-on. Out of my sight!

LULU. I'm going.

> *She exits.* MCCANN *goes to the door, left, and goes out. He ushers in* STANLEY, *who is dressed in a dark well cut suit and white collar. He holds his broken glasses in his hand. He is clean-shaven.* MCCANN *follows and closes the door.* GOLDBERG *meets* STANLEY, *seats him in a chair.*

GOLDBERG. How are you, Stan?

> *Pause.*

Are you feeling any better?

> *Pause.*

What's the matter with your glasses?

> GOLDBERG *bends to look.*

They're broken. A pity.

> STANLEY *stares blankly at the floor.*

MCCANN (*at the table*). He looks better, doesn't he?

GOLDBERG. Much better.

MCCANN. A new man.

GOLDBERG. You know what we'll do?

MCCANN. What?

GOLDBERG. We'll buy him another pair.

They begin to woo him, gently and with relish. During the
following sequence STANLEY *shows no reaction. He remains,*
with no movement, where he sits.

MCCANN. Out of our own pockets.

GOLDBERG. It goes without saying. Between you and me,
Stan, it's about time you had a new pair of glasses.

MCCANN. You can't see straight.

GOLDBERG. It's true. You've been cockeyed for years.

MCCANN. Now you're even more cockeyed.

GOLDBERG. He's right. You've gone from bad to worse.

MCCANN. Worse than worse.

GOLDBERG. You need a long convalescence.

MCCANN. A change of air.

GOLDBERG. Somewhere over the rainbow.

MCCANN. Where angels fear to tread.

GOLDBERG. Exactly.

MCCANN. You're in a rut.

GOLDBERG. You look anaemic.

MCCANN. Rheumatic.

GOLDBERG. Myopic.

MCCANN. Epileptic.

GOLDBERG. You're on the verge.

MCCANN. You're a dead duck.

GOLDBERG. But we can save you.

MCCANN. From a worse fate.

GOLDBERG. True.

MCCANN. Undeniable.

GOLDBERG. From now on, we'll be the hub of your wheel.

MCCANN. We'll renew your season ticket.

GOLDBERG. We'll take tuppence off your morning tea.

MCCANN. We'll give you a discount on all inflammable goods.

GOLDBERG. We'll watch over you.

MCCANN. Advise you.

GOLDBERG. Give you proper care and treatment.

MCCANN. Let you use the club bar.

GOLDBERG. Keep a table reserved.

MCCANN. Help you acknowledge the fast days.

GOLDBERG. Bake you cakes.

MCCANN. Help you kneel on kneeling days.

GOLDBERG. Give you a free pass.

MCCANN. Take you for constitutionals.

GOLDBERG. Give you hot tips.

MCCANN. We'll provide the skipping rope.

GOLDBERG. The vest and pants.

MCCANN. The ointment.

GOLDBERG. The hot poultice.

MCCANN. The fingerstall.

GOLDBERG. The abdomen belt.

MCCANN. The ear plugs.

GOLDBERG. The baby powder.

MCCANN. The back scratcher.

GOLDBERG. The spare tyre.

MCCANN. The stomach pump.

GOLDBERG. The oxygen tent.

MCCANN. The prayer wheel.

GOLDBERG. The plaster of Paris.

MCCANN. The crash helmet.

GOLDBERG. The crutches.

MCCANN. A day and night service.

GOLDBERG. All on the house.

MCCANN. That's it.

GOLDBERG. We'll make a man of you.

MCCANN. And a woman.

GOLDBERG. You'll be re-orientated.

MCCANN. You'll be rich.

GOLDBERG. You'll be adjusted.

MCCANN. You'll be our pride and joy.

GOLDBERG. You'll be a mensch.

MCCANN. You'll be a success.

GOLDBERG. You'll be integrated.

MCCANN. You'll give orders.

GOLDBERG. You'll make decisions.

MCCANN. You'll be a magnate.

GOLDBERG. A statesman.

MCCANN. You'll own yachts.

GOLDBERG. Animals.

MCCANN. Animals.

> GOLDBERG *looks at* MCCANN.

GOLDBERG. I said animals. (*He turns back to* STANLEY.) You'll be able to make or break, Stan. By my life. (*Silence.* STANLEY *is still.*) Well? What do you say?

> STANLEY'S *head lifts very slowly and turns in* GOLD-BERG'S *direction.*

GOLDBERG. What do you think? Eh, boy?

> STANLEY *begins to clench and unclench his eyes.*

MCCANN. What's your opinion, sir? Of this prospect, sir?

GOLDBERG. Prospect. Sure. Sure it's a prospect.

> STANLEY'S *hands clutching his glasses begin to tremble.*

What's your opinion of such a prospect? Eh, Stanley?

> STANLEY *concentrates, his mouth opens, he attempts to speak, fails and emits sounds from his throat.*

STANLEY. Uh-gug . . . uh-gug . . . eeehhh-gag . . . (*On the breath.*) Caahh . . . caahh. . . .

> *They watch him. He draws a long breath which shudders down his body. He concentrates.*

GOLDBERG. Well, Stanny boy, what do you say, eh?

> *They watch. He concentrates. His head lowers, his chin draws into his chest, he crouches.*

STANLEY. Ug-gughh . . . uh-gughhh. . . .

MCCANN. What's your opinion, sir?

STANLEY. Caaahhh . . . caaahhh. . . .

MCCANN. Mr Webber! What's your opinion?

GOLDBERG. What do you say, Stan? What do you think of the prospect?

MCCANN. What's your opinion of the prospect?

> STANLEY'S *body shudders, relaxes, his head drops, he becomes still again, stooped.* PETEY *enters from door, downstage, left.*

GOLDBERG. Still the same old Stan. Come with us. Come on, boy.

MCCANN. Come along with us.

PETEY. Where are you taking him?

> *They turn. Silence.*

GOLDBERG. We're taking him to Monty.

PETEY. He can stay here.

GOLDBERG. Don't be silly.

PETEY. We can look after him here.

GOLDBERG. Why do you want to look after him?

PETEY. He's my guest.

GOLDBERG. He needs special treatment.

PETEY. We'll find someone.

GOLDBERG. No. Monty's the best there is. Bring him, McCann.

> *They help* STANLEY *out of the chair. They all three move towards the door, left.*

PETEY. Leave him alone!

> *They stop.* GOLDBERG *studies him.*

GOLDBERG (*insidiously*). Why don't you come with us, Mr Boles?

MCCANN. Yes, why don't you come with us?

GOLDBERG. Come with us to Monty. There's plenty of room in the car.

PETEY makes no move. They pass him and reach the door. MCCANN opens the door and picks up the suitcases.

PETEY (*broken*). Stan, don't let them tell you what to do!

They exit.

Silence. PETEY stands. The front door slams. Sound of a car starting. Sound of a car going away. Silence. PETEY slowly goes to the table. He sits on a chair, left. He picks up the paper and opens it. The strips fall to the floor. He looks down at them. MEG comes past the window and enters by the back door. PETEY studies the front page of the paper.

MEG (*coming downstage*). The car's gone.

PETEY. Yes.

MEG. Have they gone?

PETEY. Yes.

MEG. Won't they be in for lunch?

PETEY. No.

MEG. Oh, what a shame. (*She puts her bag on the table.*) It's hot out. (*She hangs her coat on a hook.*) What are you doing?

PETEY. Reading.

MEG. Is it good?

PETEY. All right.

She sits by the table.

MEG. Where's Stan?

Pause.

Is Stan down yet, Petey?

PETEY. No . . . he's. . . .

MEG. Is he still in bed?

PETEY. Yes, he's . . . still asleep.

MEG. Still? He'll be late for his breakfast.
PETEY. Let him . . . sleep.

Pause.

MEG. Wasn't it a lovely party last night?
PETEY. I wasn't there.
MEG. Weren't you?
PETEY. I came in afterwards.
MEG. Oh.

Pause.

It was a lovely party. I haven't laughed so much for years.
We had dancing and singing. And games. You should have
been there.
PETEY. It was good, eh?

Pause.

MEG. I was the belle of the ball.
PETEY. Were you?
MEG. Oh yes. They all said I was.
PETEY. I bet you were, too.
MEG. Oh, it's true. I was.

Pause.

I know I was.

Curtain

Notes

(These notes are intended for use by overseas students as well as by English-born readers.)

Act I

9 *left* — left as seen from the stage facing the audience, but right from the audience's point of view.

9 *down . . . up* — 'down' is towards the front of the stage, 'up' towards the back of the stage.

9 *kitchen hatch* — window-like opening for serving food, between kitchen and dining room.

9 *cornflakes* — a common cereal breakfast food.

10 *old chairs* — 'old' expresses familiarity, has nothing to do with the chairs' age. This is the first indication of Petey's work as a deck-chair attendant, employed by the local authority to rent out deck-chairs to visitors to the beach.

11 *fried bread* — bread fried in animal fat — a tasty but not particularly nourishing food: a 'proper' hot breakfast would normally include bacon and/or egg.

12 *put them up* — find them accommodation for the night.

12 *boarding house* — lodgings, also serving meals: cheaper than hotels.

12 *on the list* — one of the boarding houses approved and 'listed' by the local council for the use of tourists. But it could be any list, including a list held by Goldberg and McCann.

13 *the Palace* — typical name for a theatre built in the late-Victorian or Edwardian period.

13 *the pier* — many seaside towns have piers (boarded walks supported on iron girders above sea level) large enough to hold a theatre, usually for variety or light musical shows.

14 *it says so* — i.e., in the manufacturer's advertisement, or on the packet.

15 *off* — sour.

15 *the front* — the promenade immediately alongside the sea shore.

17 *succulent* — juicy and delicious. In spite of the similarity to 'suckle' the word normally has no erotic or obscene overtones, but most often occurs on restaurant menus.

17 *Say please* — this would normally be used only as a reminder to young children.

18 *the strap* — belt or other strip of leather used for corporal punishment in English schools.

19 *needs papering* — needs new wallpaper.

21 *taking the Michael* — a variation on the slang phrase 'taking the Mickey' — teasing annoyingly, playing a deflating joke.

21 *Who do you think you're talking to?* — used rhetorically as an assertion of status, implying, 'you are not speaking to me respectfully or politely enough'.

21 *Mrs. Boles* — compared with their friendly relationship earlier in the scene, this is a surprisingly formal way of addressing her.

22 *all found* — board and lodging provided free.

22 *Lower Edmonton* — an outer suburb of north London, not the sort of area for an important concert.

23 *dropped him a card* — sent him a postcard — a more casual approach than a letter.

23 *the lot* — everything suitable to the occasion.

23 *carved me up* — usually, beat me up: here, apparently, 'ruined all my plans deliberately'.

23 *pulled a fast one* — tricked me.

23 *All right, Jack* — expression of defiance (no connection with 'I'm all right, Jack', a phrase asserting selfish complacency).

23 *take a tip* — understand a hint (no connection with 'tip' meaning gratuity, as on p. 32).

23 *pay a visit* — go to the lavatory. Meg is implying that Stanley is constipated.

25 *Lulu* — usually a nickname, suggesting sexiness.

25 *under her feet* — getting in her way, because he's in the house all day instead of out working.

26 *a bit of a washout* — disappointingly useless, a failure.

26 *Goldberg* — a 'typically' Jewish name.

26 *McCann* — a 'typically' Irish name.

27 *take a seat* — sit down.

27 *Do yourself a favour* — Jewish colloquial expression: indulge yourself, learn what is good for you.

27 *yet* — emphasises statement; Jewish colloquial.

27 *Brighton* — a very popular, sometimes vulgar, seaside resort.

27 *Canvey Island* — site of an oil refinery, hence incongruous in this context.

27 *Rottingdean* — a quiet south coast seaside resort, favoured by elderly, retired people. Like Brighton and Canvey Island, convenient for one-day trips from London.

27 *Shabbuss* — Sabbath, the Jewish day of rest.

27 *One of the old school* — one following traditional, usually stricter, conventions. The implications are favourable.

27 *Basingstoke* — large, nondescript English town, with a slightly comic name.

28 *Culture? Don't talk to me about culture* — emphasises that Goldberg's culture cannot be questioned: Jewish colloquial.

28 *what do you mean?* — emphasises preceding statement: Jewish colloquial.

28 *coppers* — coins of low value.

28 *M.C.C.* — Marylebone Cricket Club, now the headquarters of English cricket. M.C.C. was also the name used by the English cricket team when playing other than test matches abroad — hence Goldberg's reference.

28 *my name was good* — credit would be given because of Goldberg's name and reputation alone, without any other guarantee.

28 *do a job* — 'job' in this phrase usually has criminal overtones.

28 *all over the place* — nervous, over-excited, lacking self-control.

28 *cool as a whistle* — in perfect self-control.

32 *give him a tip* — a 'tip' is a gratuity, given for service, quite inappropriate for a concert pianist. Meg has misunderstood 'take a tip', p. 32.

33 *down in the dumps* — depressed.

Act II

37 *Many happy returns of the day* — conventional birthday greeting.

38 *everything's laid on* — everything is already organized or prepared.

38 *'The Mountains of Morne'* — popular, sentimental Irish song.

38 *booze-up* — common drinking party.

39 *Maidenhead* — a large middle-class English town on the River Thames. The name offers scope for sexual innuendo.

39 *Fuller's teashop* — one of a chain of respectable, old-fashioned tea-shops, superior to cheap cafés. No longer in existence.

39 *Boots Library* — one of the chain of small lending libraries run by Boots, the chemists. A small fee was paid for each book borrowed, giving the libraries a social standing 'superior' to that of the much larger but free public libraries. No longer in existence.

41 *Round the bend* — crazy.

41 *leading you up the garden path* — deliberately deceiving you.

42 *what you're at* — what you mean.

42 *Basingstoke* — (see note on p. 27).

42 *they respect the truth* — the Irish are popularly supposed to be more imaginative than strictly truthful.

42 *they have a sense of humour* — the Irish are popularly renowned as objects of jokes concerning their supposed upside-down logic.

42 *I think their policemen are wonderful* this is a compliment frequently paid by tourists to British (not Irish) policemen.

42 *draught Guinness* — Guinness, the strong Irish stout, was widely exported in bottles, but was less widely available in England on draught (from barrels) at this time.

43 *had the pleasure* — had the pleasure of meeting him before.

43 *a walk down the canal* — lovers in cities would often walk along quiet canal-side paths.

43 *bird* — girl (slang).

43 *Sunday school teacher* — many Christian churches run Sunday school classes for religious teaching, often taught by well-meaning young ladies of the neighbourhood.

43 *give her a peck* — give her a little kiss.

43 *dog stadium* — arena for greyhound racing — a commercialised feature of urban life out of keeping with the romantic sunset.

43 *Carrikmacross* — town in Monaghan, in the Republic of Ireland.

43 *gefilte fish* — popular Jewish dish.

44 *Don't mess me about* — don't interfere with me.

44 *We're booked out* — all accommodation has already been taken.

44 *game* — here, a way of making money, with implications of dishonesty.

45 *boghouse* — lavatory.

45 *unlicensed premises* — a licence is necessary for restaurants, etc., where the public go to buy and consume alcoholic drinks, but is not of course necessary for private parties in a private house. If the house really is a boarding house, then a licence would be needed for a drinking party.

45 *isn't your cup of tea* — isn't what you like, isn't suitable for you.

45 *from any angle* — in any way.

46 *get on my breasts* — a slightly politer form of the vulgar 'get on my tits' — irritate me. Not used in polite conversation.

47 *kick the shite out of him* — injure him (a general threat).

47 *getting on everybody's wick* — irritating and annoying everybody.

47 *off her conk* — off her head, mad.

48 *the organization* — the implication is of a Mafia-like criminal network.

48 *Black and Tan* — 'Black and Tans' was the nickname given to an irregular force of British soldiers sent to repress the 'troubles' in Ireland from 1919 to 1922, notorious for the brutality of their methods. 'Black and Tan' is not usually used adjectivally, but here evidently implies general hostility.

48 *on the wrong horse* — mistaken: the connotations are of betting on a horse race.

48 *Enos or Andrews* — brand names of two kinds of sparkling fruit salts (patent medicines for stomach upsets).

49 *Lyons Corner House* — one of the chain of large, multiple restaurants which existed in London until recently — places for respectable, middle-class family eating.

49 *Marble Arch* — in central London at the western end of Oxford Street. A Lyons Corner House used to exist there.

49 *waiting at the porch* — waiting at the church porch, as a bride whose groom has not arrived.

49 *skedaddled* — ran away.

50 *left her in the lurch* — abandoned her while she was in trouble.

50 *in the pudding club* — pregnant.

50 *waiting at the church* — this and 'left her in the lurch' are lines from an old music-hall comic song.

50 *Joe Soap* — derisive name implying 'nobody who matters'.

50 *possible or necessary* — the passage which follows uses the philosophical jargon of local positivism, abruptly changing tone with Goldberg's first speech on p. 51.

51 *all along the line* — in every respect.

51 *What about Ireland* — Ireland has a long history of exploitation and violence at the hands of the English (see also 'Black and Tan', p. 48, and 'Drogheda', p. 53).

51 *building society* — a company which makes loans to those wishing to purchase their own home.

51 *a traitor to the cloth* — someone who has done something to undermine his status as a priest, 'the cloth' being the vestments of a clergyman.

51 *Albigensenist heresy* — belief in a principal of evil as well as of good, which denied the divinity of Christ. The Albigensenist heretics were mostly massacred, and their sect destroyed.

51 *watered the wicket at Melbourne* — the wicket (the playing area in cricket) was probably illegally watered on the night of 1 January or during 2 January, 1955, between the second and third day's play in the third Test match between England and Australia at Melbourne. The effect of the watering was to reduce the speed of the ball and to make it bounce more predictably off the pitch, in the apparent hope of aiding the Australian cricketers, who had to bat last. The issue of 'who watered the wicket?' was widely discussed in newspapers for a few days.

51 *the blessed Oliver Plunkett* — the last of the Irish religious martyrs.

51 *Why did the chicken cross the road?* — A very well-known joke, its point being that the answer — 'because it wanted to get to the other side' — is not clever but an anti-climax.

52 *Which came first?* — A very well-known riddle that has no answer: 'Which came first, the chicken or the egg?' Often quoted with reference to complex, interdependent problems.

52 *Drogheda* — Irish town, site of a notorious massacre of the inhabitants by the English general, Cromwell, in 1649.

52 *an overthrow* — in cricket, a ball thrown back too far by a fielder, sometimes resulting in a run (a point) being scored by the other side.

53 *Enough to scuttle a liner* — enough liquid to sink a large ship.

53 *Scotch . . . Irish* — Scotch whisky and Irish whiskey (the different spelling is carefully preserved).

53 *in the business* — in the dressmaking business — a 'typically' Jewish occupation.

54 *Walk up the boulevard* — walk along proudly as if on a fashionable boulevard (avenue).

54 *turn about and promenade* — the sort of instructions called out during the already unfashionable American square dance.

54 *Gladiola* — Goldberg's coinage of a feminine form of 'gladiolus' (usual plural, 'gladioli'), a kind of flower.

54 *it's all yours* — everyone is attending to you.

55 *'Hear — hear'* — conventional exclamation of agreement during a public speech.

55 *smile at the birdy* — traditionally said by photographers to attract the attention of their subjects, especially children.

56 *Gone with the wind* — title of an enormously successful

American popular novel and feature film — here, simply implying 'vanished'.

56 *little Austin* — a modest car, at one time very common.

56 *Fullers . . . Boots* — (see notes on p. 39).

56 *on our tod* — alone; a slang phrase out of keeping with the rest of his 'philosophical' remark.

56 *to kip on* — to sleep on: again, the slang term is out of keeping with the serious sentiment.

56 *Mazoltov* — Congratulations; conventional Jewish greeting.

56 *Simchahs* — a Jewish holiday.

57 *well over the fast* — Jewish form of salutation.

57 *Ethical Hall, Bayswater* — Lecture hall in an unfashionable part of West London.

57 *Charlotte Street* — a street north of Soho in London, best known for its many foreign restaurants.

57 *It went like a bomb* — it was a great success.

57 *speak at weddings* — traditionally a series of speeches are made at wedding celebrations, on light personal topics.

58 *mix that stuff* — that is, mix the Scotch and Irish whiskies. In fact it is all whisky but McCann feels that Irish whiskey is so unlike (and presumably superior to) the Scotch that he regards it as another kind of drink.

59 *Carrikmacross* — (see note on P. 43).

59 *King's Cross* — main line railway station in London for northern destinations.

59 *out of the blue* — unexpectedly.

59 *Gesundheit* — German (and Jewish) toast, or greeting when drinking, etc.

59 *constitutional* — a walk taken for one's health.

59 *rollmop and pickled cucumber* — popularly favoured Jewish delicacy.

60 *piggy-back* — giving a ride on one's back, usually to a child.

60 *pop goes the weasel* — climax to an old music-hall song and nursery rhyme.

60 *Roscrea* — small town in Tipperary, in the Republic of Ireland.

60 *Mother Nolan's* — presumably a bar in Roscrea.

60 *Tullamore* — town in Offaly in the Republic of Ireland.

60 *Fenian men* — name adopted during the nineteenth century for fighters for Irish freedom from British rule.

61 *The night that poor Paddy was stretched* — a Dublin street-ballad. 'Stretched' means hanged. The song is hardly 'a love song'.

61 *Oh, the Garden of Eden* — popular Irish ballad.
61 *Hide and seek* — a children's game.
61 *Blind man's buff* — a children's game, played as enacted in the text below.
65 *spread-eagled* — flat out with arms and legs outstretched. There are implications of torture and/or sexual gratification in the relative positions of Lulu and Stanley.

Act III

67 *slept like a log* — slept very soundly.
70 *next to no time* — almost at once.
71 *a few letters after his name* — that is, letters indicating professional qualifications.
71 *pure and simple* — only this, without complications.
72 *Abdullah* — a brand of Egyptian cigarettes.
72 *shilling in the slot* — the electricity supply is in some houses controlled by a coin-operated meter: a coin (at this period, often a shilling) had to be placed in the meter, and bought a certain amount of electricity, after which the electricity would be cut off unless another coin was inserted.
74 *Sellotape* — brand name of a transparent, self-adhesive tape.
75 *My life* — an emphatic exclamation: Jewish colloquial.
76 *get it over* — finish it quickly.
76 *knocked out* — exhausted.
77 *fit as a fiddle* — very healthy.
77 *Play up, play up, and play the game* — climax to poetic celebration of public school values. From a poem by Henry Newbolt, once popular as a recitation piece.
77 *Honour thy father and thy mother* — the fifth of the ten commandments given by God in the Old Testament of the Bible (Exodus 20, 12). Out of keeping with the cricketing metaphor before, and the colloquialism following.
77 *All along the line* — constantly and consistently (cf. note on p. 51).
77 *kept my eye on the ball* — always paid close attention; another cricketing metaphor.
77 *follow my line? Follow my mental?* — do you follow my train of thought, the course of my argument?
77 *don't go too near the water* — always be cautious, not reckless: advice commonly given by over-anxious parents to children.
78 *schnorrers* — beggars: Jewish colloquial.

78 *Work hard and play hard* — conventional advice given by schoolteachers to children.

79 *You got the needle to* — Do you feel hostile towards?

79 *pontoon* — a card game, played for money, also called vingt-et-un.

79 *Do you think I'm like all the other girls?* — a banal, conventional reproach often found in cheap fiction.

80 *Lulu, schmulu* — typical Jewish wordplay, implying that the difference of opinion is not important.

80 *do me a turn* — do me a favour (implying, see the sense of what I'm saying).

80 *You used me for a night. A passing fancy* — clichés used following seduction scenes in cheap fiction.

80 *a jump ahead* — in a superior position of knowledge and experience.

80 *to confess* — the Irish Republic, from which McCann evidently comes, is a Roman Catholic country, and the confession (and absolution) of sins is a requirement of the Roman Catholic church.

81 *tell me the latest* — that is, the latest news or gossip: colloquial, not appropriate to a confession.

81 *Rock of Cashel* — Irish beauty spot where several ruins stand on a conspicuous crag.

82 *out of our own pockets* — that is, the money will come 'out of our own pockets'.

82 *cockeyed* — confused and mistaken.

82 *A change of air* — conventionally recommended by doctors for nervous ailments.

82 *Somewhere over the rainbow* — first line of a popular song, suggesting an unattainable place (or ambition).

82 *Where angels fear to tread* — from the well-known proverb: 'Fools rush in where angels fear to tread' (originally from a couplet by Pope).

82 *You're in a rut* — you are too fixed in a routine.

82 *You're on the verge* — something dangerous (e.g. madness) is imminent.

82 *You're a dead duck* — your fate is decided.

82 *renew your season ticket* — a wise step urged by railway advertisements. A 'season' ticket permits travel for varying periods at a reduction over the equivalent daily rates.

82 *take tuppence off your morning tea . . . give you a discount* — variations on temptations offered by advertisements.

82 *proper care and treatment* — assurance of service given by a